LINES OF A Lifetime

Collected Poems

by

John Coutts

Best wishes
John Coutts

i

ISBN 978-1-871828-70-2

British Library Cataloguing in Publication Data:
A catalogue record for this publication is available from the British Library

Typeset in 11pt Garamond

Printed in Scotland by Westport Print, St Andrews

Illustrations by Margaret Stein

Handsel Press

Avalon, 35 Dunbar Rd, Haddington EH41 3PJ

CONTENTS

TALES FROM THE PAST

VOICES FROM THE PAST

PEOPLE AND PLACES

A BUNCH OF VALENTINES

WEDDING GIFTS

THANKSGIVINGS

CHRISTMAS INTERPRETED

EASTER INTERPRETED

A HANDFUL OF HYMNS

AN OFFERING OF PRAYER

TRANSLATIONS

ENCOUNTER WITH PUSHKIN

YOUNG PUSHKIN

PUSHKIN THE POET OF LOVE

VERSATILE PUSHKIN

PUSHKIN THE NARRATIVE POET

PUSHKIN THE DRAMATIC POET

PUSHKIN THE VISIONARY

PUSHKIN THE FRIEND

PUSHKIN THE ENEMY

POEMS IN SCOTS

AND FINALLY

PREFACE

The poems in this book were written over many years, for a variety of readers and listeners both old and young. The author values the skills that have graced English poetry over many centuries, and makes use of a wide variety of metrical forms, from classical blank verse to contemporary rap.

Included are a number of poems in Scots, as well as translations from French, Greek, German and Russian.

MAINLY FOR CHILDREN

EVERYCHILD . . .

Good or greedy, tame or wild,
Any child is Everychild.

I'm the boy from long ago,
Hunting deer with spear and bow.

I'm the girl from far away:
In my dreams you come to play.

I'm behind your garden wall:
Could you let me have my ball?

I'm the wise and winning one –
Fab at games and full of fun.

I went missing: were you there?
I was Taken Into Care.

I am brown or white or black,
Lying ill on mother's back,

Far too weak for treats or tricks:
I have legs like brittle sticks.

Did you see me on TV?
Won't you take me on your knee?

Good or greedy, tame or wild,
Any child is Everychild.

ON THE BEACH

Plastic windmills
Whirling round;
Ghetto blasters'
Bellowing sound;
Candy floss
All pink and sticky;
Trays with tea-cups
(Very tricky)
Camera missing –
Under the heap . . .
Uncle William
Fast asleep.

AN EIGHTH BIRTHDAY POEM

She started at none;
But then she was one.
She wriggled and grew
Until she was two.
After which – you'll agree –
She just had to be three.
It was twelve months before
She made it to four.
When five – so I'm told –
She was sixty months old.
The clock tick-tock-ticks . . .
And soon she is six.
She was seven a whole year . . .
Get ready to cheer!
May the Third is the date
When our Bridie is EIGHT!
Shout hip-hip-hooray.
O fabulous day!
I'll do better next time.
I'VE RUN OUT OF RHYME.

POEMS ABOUT POEMS

THE ONOMATOPOEIA POEM

Dong - ding - ding - dong -
(Sounding words can sing a song.)
Twitter - cackle - hoot - screech -
(Speaking words can tell and teach.)
Whizz - buzz - hum - zoom -
(An angry wasp invades my room.)
Creaks - bangs - clattering crashes -
(A tray slips - a bottle smashes.)
Howl - growl - snuffle - bark -
(Something's out there in the dark.)
Giggle - mutter - mumble - cough -
(Time to switch this poem off!)

THE REMEMBER-YOUR-RHYTHM POEM

Slow , slow , quick - quick - slow,
Grandma's dance would sway and flow.
But the rap and the rhythm get a grip on your feet
In the flash-bang club where the ravers meet . . .
" It's much too loud: I'll go to bed and dream
Of Shakespeare plays where thoughts run round the ends
of lines – like this: "
"One kiss! One kiss!
Romeo, Romeo, king of humanity!"
"Juliet, my dearest one, this is insanity!
For a horrible man in in the very front row
Has been sucking a sweet since the start of the show."
Slow , slow , quick - quick - slow . . .

THE RHYME POEM

Words that rhyme:
Swing and chime
Just like bells,
Ding-dong-ding!
Rhyme can sing:
Rhyming tells
You when to laugh, to clap to cry . . .
Just you try!
Rhyme keeps time
Slow or quick;
Tick - tock - tick
Tock - tick - tock.
Rhyme can shock . . .
Rhyme can mix magic and rhyme can experiment;
Rhyme can be tragic and rhyme can cause merriment.
Rhyming teaches – rhyming makes clear;
Rhymes were used by William Shake - speare . . .

GROANS!

Dear oh dear!
That's enough!
Rhyming's tough.
If you rhyme,
All the time,
Feeble verse
Gets worse
And worse . . .
And worse . . .

ELSPETH GIVES GRANDPA A DANCING LESSON
(more rhythms)

One-two-three . . . One-two-three . . . One-two-three . . . One!
Grandpa, do dance with me! Join in the fun!
One   AND   two   AND   one   AND   two . . .
Let - me - show - you - what - to - do . . .
One-two-three-four-one-two-three . . .
Try - to - move - your - feet - like - me!
ONE two three . . . TWO two three . . . ONE two three . . .
  TWO two three.
Elspeth, I'm sorry – this dancing is new to me!
Slow – slow – quick - quick - slow . . .
Stop it, Grandpa . . . No . . . No . . . No!
ONE two three – TWO two three – that's how it goes . . .
Grandpa, be careful! You trod on my toes!
ONE two three . . . FOUR five six . . . SEVEN eight nine . . .
  TEN!
O what a muddle! Let's do it again!

THE DOODLEBUG

(A 'doodlebug' was a flying bomb – a pilotless plane – in the Second World War. Once the engine cut out, the plane would crash and the bomb explode.)

Droning – droning
High in the sky,
Droning – droning
The doodlebugs fly.

Doodlebug comes,
And doodlebugs go;
Bombs up there,
And people down below.

Droning – droning
High in the sky,
Droning – droning
The doodlebugs fly.

Droning . . . droning . . .
Hiding in a cloud;
Here comes the doodlebug
Getting very loud!

Droning us to death . . .   (slow down!)
When the engine stops
You can hold your breath
As the doodlebug drops.   (pause!)

"Please, dear God,
Do hear my prayer;
Make it crash
On any-old-where.
Or dump it in a field
When nobody's there."

Droning – droning
High in the sky.
Droning – droning
The doodlebugs fly.

Droning . . . droning . . .
Fading away,
Nasty doodlebug
Didn't come to stay.
Cheerio, doodlebug!
I'm not dead.
My mum says
"Let's go back to bed."

Droning – droning
High in the sky.
Droning – droning
The doodlebugs fly.

.

WHAT IS BABY THINKING?

Baby   Young and light and good to throw . . .
Grown-up That's a saucer. Let it go.

Baby   Shivery-shiny, clear and cool . . .
Grown-up Darling, don't go near the pool.

Baby   Splashing, sliding down my skin . . .
Grown-up Baby mustn't tumble in.

Baby   Feeling nice inside my nose . . .
Grown-up No - it's wrong to eat a rose . . .

Baby   Up and up towards the top . . .
Grown-up Dearie me – when will it stop?

Baby   Squishy-squashy – is this right?
Grown-up Muddy fingers – what a sight . . .

Grown-up Bed-time now – and do not yell!
Baby   NO . . . NO . . . NO . . . NO . . . oh well . . .

STARTING SCHOOL

There it is:
Behind the gate!
He went in.
I think I'll wait.

Monday morning . . .
Bright and cool:
Must I really
Go to school?

Girls go laughing
One - two - three.
No one seemed
To notice me.

Someone said
They pick on you . . .
How I hope
It isn't true.

There's a teacher
Looking grim:
Please, dear God,
I don't want HIM!

Is it soft
To miss your mum?
Now I wish
I'd let her come.

Mustn't lose
My dinner money . . .
Tie's too tight . . .
My legs feel funny . . .

There's the bell . . .
Jing - jangly loud . . .
Time to join
The shoving crowd.

Some look just
As scared as me . . .
One deep breath:
Count up to three . . .

Slip inside . . .
"New school, hello!
Howdee, stranger . . .
Friend or foe?"

COME TO THE WOODS!

(A treat for the Five Senses)

Come to the woods:
The sudden storm
Has done its work.
The air is warm.

Grey-green beech trees . . .
See them stand
Like lords above
A living land.

Bluebells raise
Their heads again.
Smell the soil
Refreshed by rain.

Something rustled:
Did you hear?
Maybe a timid
Mouse is near.

Mind your legs!
Beware of nettles . . .
Stroke the face
Of primrose petals.

Hawthorn leaves
Are good to chew:
It's "bread and cheese".
You taste it too!

Touch and see
And hear and smell:
The woods are yours,
And all is well.

When I was young hawthorn leaves really were known as 'bread and cheese'

DAYDREAMING

How long does it take
To fly to a star?
Is it cold? Is it lonely
And fearsome and far?

Our school is let out
At something past three.
Could you stop off on Mars
And be home before tea?

I lay on my back:
The sky was so near.
A long blade of grass
Tried to tickle my ear...

It seemed the right time
To climb into my rocket.
But then I discovered
A hole in my pocket.

So countdown was cancelled:
I jumped to my feet.
The van that sells ices
Ding-donged in our street.

You can fly to the moon
In a thought, in a dream:
But O for the money
To buy an ice-cream!

AUTUMN SONG

Smooth to rough
And green to gold:
April buds
Are growing old.

Lithe to brittle,
Gold to brown;
Summer's necklace
Flutters down.

Shivering trees
Look old and ill:
Rub your fingers
Sniff the chill.

Hurry up!
It's getting dark.
There's the man
Who locks the park.

Stroke a dry
And bony leaf:
Stop a minute:
Share the grief.

Summer's song
Is nearly sung...
Don't be daft;
I'm tough, I'm young.

Crack the twig
And slash the fern.
Welcome, Winter!
Take your turn.

Watch me kick
Dead leaves away:
Spring will soon
Come out to play.

Smooth to rough
And green to gold,
April buds
Are growing old.

JOHN O'GROATS

The northern tip of Scotland is named after Jan de Groot, a Dutch seaman. King James IV appointed him to set up a ferry to Orkney in 1497.

John o'Groats . . .
Who on earth were you?
And how did you get your name on the map?
You must have been a remarkable chap.
They say you had something do with boats –
Is this true –
John o'Groats?

"Jan de Groot!"
– King James decreed –
"We need a new ferry to cross the sea,
For the Orkney Islands belong to me!
This Dutchman's a sailor of high repute.
The man we need
Is Jan de Groot!"

*From 'Groot' to 'Groats': to 'John' from 'Jan' . . .
That's how the magical name began.*

13

LAND'S END

Land's End –
The wind sings:
Grasses shake;
The rain stings.

Land's End –
I'm near the edge:
Seagulls perch
On rock and ledge . . .

Land's End –
The waves come
And come again . . .
"It's all right, mum."

Land's End –
A broken box
Slides and bumps
Against the rocks.

Lands End –
Sea and sky!
Can you hear me
Shout "Goodbye"?

Will you let me
Be your friend –
Wild and lonely
Land's End?

THE SECRET POOL
(a spell broken)

Tide, tide,
Slither and slide:
Leave the pool
Clear and cool
Where secret aliens hide . . .

Where I –
So high –
Can spy
Another planet far below:
Seaweed waving
Green and slow;
A shrimp swimming
Frantic and fast;
A crab marching
Solemnly past;
A limpet clinging
To slimy stone . . .

Can that be a fish
The colour of sand?

Alone on the rocks
I'm far from land

I watch my world for a long, long minute . . .
And then I PUT MY FOOT RIGHT IN IT . . .

Tide, tide,
Slither and slide:
Cover the pool –
Clear and cool –
Where silent aliens hide.

THE PULL-AND-PUSH

A poem for everybody

The rhythm is ONE - TWO - THREE - FOUR. We have marked
two lines to help you get started.

1	2	3	4

Sh - sh - sh — pull-and-push: pull-and-push.
Sh - sh - sh — pull-and-push: pull-and-push.

        1   2   3   4

There's a funny old train on a single track
Pulling you there and pushing you back.
A couple of coaches – that's enough
To make the engine hiss and puff.

Sh - sh - sh — pull-and-push: pull-and-push.
Sh - sh - sh — pull-and-push: pull-and-push.

After school – if you run very fast –
You will see Pull-and-Push go rattling past.
Stand on the gate and wave – that's fine:
But never never walk on the railway line.

(WHISTLE!)

Sh - sh - sh — pull-and-push: pull-and-push.
Sh - sh - sh — pull-and-push: pull-and-push.

Wait on the bridge at the end of the lane.
Here comes Pull-and-Push puffing back again!
Up from below comes a cloud of smoke.
Stand well back or you'll cough and choke.

Sh - sh - sh – pull-and-push: pull-and-push.
Sh - sh - sh – pull-and-push: pull-and-push.

What's it like if you sit inside?
Tuppence for a ticket! Come for a ride!
Smuts from the funnel are flying on the breeze –
Don't lean out of the window – please:

(WHISTLE AGAIN!)

Sh - sh - sh – pull-and-push: pull-and-push.
Sh - sh - sh – pull-and-push: pull-and-push.

This was a train of long, long ago:
Grandpa told me: he should know.
(I think Grandpa likes to dream
Of days of fun and whistles and steam . . .)

SLOW DOWN, PLEASE:
(ONE MORE WHISTLE)

Sh - sh - sh – pull-and-push: pull-and-push.
Sh - sh - sh – pull-and-push: pull-and-push.

(SLOW DOWN AND STOP)

Sh - sh - sh – pull-and-push: pull-and-push.
Sh - sh - sh – pull-and-push: pull-and-push.

The 'Pull-and-Push' was a train that ran from Watford Junction to St Albans Abbey Station.

AMELIA'S POEM

The holidays had started,
No school! Hip hip hooray!
So early in the morning
Amelia went out to play,

She ran to the children's swing park
And what do you think she found?
A small and shiny space ship
Sat humming on the ground.

It came from a distant planet
Ten zillion miles: non-stop!
And lots of little spacelings
Peeped out of the lid on top.

Each one had a winky wotsit
On either side of its head.
If you think that they all looked funny,
Just listen to what they said:

"Inggong – balong – baboozum
Perdim – galim – fatoo".
What on earth were they trying to tell us?
Not even the grown-ups knew.

Amelia smiled – and showed them
The seesaw, swings and slides,
The climbing frame – and the Flying Fox
Which gives you exciting rides.

Then round and round the swing-park
She watched the spacelings run
They shouted "Caloogally wobobble!" *
Which possibly means "What fun!"

18

Then people started barging,
Their wotsits winked and flashed;
The Flying Fox went sideways
And somebody nearly crashed.

"Behave yourselves." said Amelia
(Like teacher, loud and clear.)
"Remember to play politely!
No pushing and shoving here."

Our visitors said "Gum-boshee."
The message was understood.
They stood in a queue as she told them to do
And tried very hard to be good.

But then a siren sounded,
The lift-off engines roared.
The spacelings chattered and muttered
And hurriedly climbed on board,

And before you could say "Jack Robinson"
(If that's what you wanted to say)
The spaceship rose and hovered
And suddenly whizzed away.

I checked with a brainy professor
To ask if he thought it probable
That people on distant planets
Say things like "Caloogally wobobble."

"Maybe" said the brainy professor.
"On the other hand – maybe not."
(Which shows what can happen to people
Who know a tremendous lot)

"Inggong – balong – baboozum
Perdim – galim – fatoo.
Gumboshee – caloogally wobobble"
I tell you my tale is true!

And if somebody says I'm a fibber,
Or calls it a "pack of lies",
Just ask them down to the swing-park.
They may get a big surprise.

* *IMPORTANT NOTE!* *"caloogally wobobble"*
  sounds like "extremely improbable".

DEAR ELSPETH

Dear Elspeth,

Today
I'm happy to say,
I opened a jar
Which came from afar
(From 'Peebles', but I'm
afraid this won't rhyme)
I was told it was jam
Prepared by your mam
And by you!
Was it true
From you – sent to me,
To enjoy for my tea?

It surprises this lover
Of jam, to discover
Not you, but your dad
Makes grandpa feel glad
With this exquisite jam!
Each delicate gram
Must be carefully spread
On toast or fresh bread.
Not eaten in haste –
For that would be waste:
(It's greedy to cram
one's mouth full of jam)

I have eaten roast yam,
Made do with tinned spam,
Spread mustard on ham
And drunk tea from Assam,
But none could compare
(I affirm and declare)
With this raspberry jam.
So I sing and I send
To you, my young friend.
This wild dithyramb. *
How happy I am!

PS: Give thanks to my son
(Your dad – that's the one)
Come and visit us soon:
We'll be over the moon.
And after exams
Could you help him make jams?

a big word! Try the dictionary.

"FIVE TO KEEP A CHILD ALIVE"

(in aid of Save The Children's 'Give us a Fiver' Campaign)

Count the pounds – and give us five.
Five to keep a child alive.

Child of hardship, please don't die:
All the world should hear you cry.

Nurse's needle made you yell:
But what she did will keep you well.

Count the pounds – and give us five.
Five to keep a child alive.

Here's a blanket: wrap up warm.
Slumber through the roaring storm,

Snug inside your net all night,
Where mosquitoes never bite.

Count the pounds – and give us five.
Five to keep a child alive.

Dirty water made you ill:
Now it's safe to drink your fill,

Peanut butter makes you strong.
Taste it. Try some more. Live long!

Count the pounds – and give us five.
Five to keep a child alive.

TALES FROM THE PAST

A MILLENNIUM MESSAGE
TO THE FUTURE
FROM AGE CONCERN GRAVESEND

(by John Coutts with the help of many friends, May 2000)

Dear Friends in the Future,
                              All hail and hello!
There are one or two things that we'd like you to know.
Our poet will pickle in rhythm and rhyme
Some views of our age, of our town and our time,
And present for your pleasure and kind contemplation
The triumphs and trials of our own generation.
We warn you! The store of our wisdom is vast,
And so we offer this helpful thought . . .
Have faith in the future and love for the past.

Let's begin at the car parks – those wide open spaces
Once crowded with houses and graced with good faces;
Five pubs on one corner, with barrels and bar:
Where are they? The Victory? The Lion? The Star?
Those bullocks who walked – unaware of their fate –
Via Beamish the butchers to oven and plate?
The Pawn Shop in Stone Street: mum slipped in on Monday
And pledged the best suit that her man wore on Sunday.
Remember! Gravesend may not be what it seems.
So lock the car gently – you park on our dreams.
Mr James had a farm – it was tended so well –
But it lies beneath bricks by the Woodlands Hotel.
And the sight of our traffic would leave him aghast...
Still, things could be worse, so . . .
Have faith in the future and love for the past.

Just how did the boys and the girls get to meet?
By parading on opposite sides of the street.
One side was 'half crown' and the other 'the shilling'.
On Sundays the monkey walk showed who was willing;
And the girls would look out for a fellow to like.
One lass caught the eye of a lad with a bike . . .
But an Arthur Street mansion was grievously dear,
So they carried on courting for many a long year,
But the troth that they plighted stuck joyfully fast
Which proves it is a good idea to
Have faith in the future and love for the past.

To Harmer Street next, where the Grand in its pride
Charged fourpence or sixpence to let you inside:
With chestnuts on sale to the posh and the poor,
That 'Murder Most Foul' was enacted once more.
And Fleapit and Gallery gasped at the Red
Barn – where Maria lay gruesomely dead.
Alas for the Grand – its walls were unsound;
By the Council's decree it was knocked to the ground [1]
When Old Father Time blew a merciless blast.
But never mind . . . you have TV – so
Have faith in the future and love for the past.

You'd expect us to mention the war, would you not?
The drone of the doodlebug choosing its spot;
Dried egg on the menu, and gasmask on hip,
And Waterdales flattened, and Everard's ship
Torpedoed at sea – but all was not over, [2]
They grounded their boat by the white cliffs of Dover.
It was thought that a medal was just the right thing.
"I'm pleased to present you with this" said the King,
For their colours of courage were nailed to the mast.
Take notice, please . . .
Have faith in the future and love for the past.

Times change. You could walk in the dark to the farm[3]
For you knew every footstep and came to no harm.
From the top of a tram you could look at the track
As it clattered from Northfleet to Denton and back.
The poor had the dosshouse – the old Ragged School
Taught reading by rote and neat writing by rule,
And down by the river the mudlarks would stand
And beg for the coppers you hid in your hand.
There are things that are simply too painful to say.
Dear Friends in the Future – rejoice in your day.
We were young and hard up, we were glad, we were sad,
We can't ever count all the fun that we had.
But life, you will find, is jam-packed with surprise,
And since we are patient – and thoughtful – and wise,
This Millennium Message is crafted to last:
Have faith in the future and love for the past.

[1] *In 1934 , so it seems.*

[2] *Captain Harry Cottam was decorated by King George VI for beaching the Motor Vessel 'Summitry' after it had been torpedoed. Everard's yard was in Greenhithe.*

[3] *In Shorne village.*

OLDBURY HILL

(an Iron Age fort near Sevenoaks, Kent, England)

Oldbury Hill is O-so-old:
In spring it's warm and green and gold.

The path is twisty: slopes are steep,
And the trees are tall and the thickets deep:

But just go back two thousand years
To a world of wolves and bears and fears:

This happy hill was a stronghold then,
With a ditch dug out by desperate men

Do you see the dip where the hollybush grows?
That was the work of women with hoes,

As children carried the earth away,
Thirsty and hot on a summer's day.

With hammer and axe and saw and spade
They crowned their hill with a strong stockade

And barred the creaking wooden gate:
But why the spears, the fears, the hate?

A child was there from long ago:
We met in the wood where the bluebells grow;

I stopped and waved to say "hello".
He drew an arrow and bent his bow . . .

I said: "I come from time-to-be.
So please, don't shoot! Do play with me."

"Why not?" he said, "But do beware.
Stop if the war-horn sounds up there.

First the horn and then the drum:
They let us know when raiders come."

I didn't feel at all afraid:
We ran and laughed in sun and shade.

For ever and ever we laughed and ran
In the very best game since the world began.

A sudden rustling stopped our play:
A fox looked up and trotted away.

Then I heard a honking horn below:
My iron-age pal just had to go.

Back in the car-park dad was cross.
He said "You kept us waiting, boss."

So now in bed I lie quite still,
And talk to my friend on Oldbury Hill.

SMALL MERCIES

(an unreported incident on the road to Bethlehem)

"There went forth a decree from Caesar Augustus that all the world should be enrolled . . . and Joseph . . . went up . . . to Bethlehem . . . to be enrolled with Mary, his betrothed, who was with child." (Luke 2:1,4)

Soldier, please, untie the gate.
Bad luck. Too late.

We've got to find a place to stay.
Sorry; no way.

Why close the road at census time?
For fear of crime.

Sir, we are poor: we tell no lies.
You could be spies.

What do we do? Sit here all night?
You've got it right.

Sir, my dear wife . . . her time is near . . .
That's very clear.

God help us! What a situation!
Try a donation.

For pity's sake! Take all I've got.
It's not a lot.

Please, soldier, take it. Won't it do?
Keep half. Go through.

Soldier, today you've saved a life.
What says the wife?

My son will bless you, sir, for showing . . . "
Weakness. Get going.

A PRAYER TO MARS THE AVENGER

*by the Roman army before battle against the forces of Boudicca,
Queen of the Britons*

Lord of battles, mighty Mars,
God who rules below the stars,

Soldiers' champion, hungry king:
Taste the sacrifice we bring!

See this harmless heifer die.
Blood for blood: Great Mars, reply!

Let the steady marching drum
Warn the foe that Romans come.

Why should gleaming eagles fear
Savage queen or charioteer?

Let the British war-horns bray.
Drill and skill shall gain the day.

When the arrows whizz and hiss
Not a stroke of ours shall miss.

Let the queen who killed our friends
Flee before the battle ends.

Grant her lords dishonoured graves:
Sell their brats as Roman slaves.

Burning barns adorn the night.
Smoke and flame is Mars' delight.

Women weep and widows wail.
Mars the Avenger cannot fail.

Give us booty, fortune, fame:
Crown the conquering Legion's name.

Hail, great Mars! Your men shall win.
Prayer is done: Let war begin.

THE MAN WHO LAID THE MOSAIC

The Roman villa at Lullingstone, Kent, features two famous mosaics: The
Four Seasons *and* The Rape of Europa *by Zeus in the shape of a bull.*

I am the man
Who came from Gaul,
Whose heart and hand
Designed it all.

I sent my slave
To name a fee;
For no-one lays
Mosaics like me.

The backward Briton
Gladly pays
To hide his rude
And savage ways;

So I, the artist
– I alone –
Laid the mosaics
In speckled stone.

That swimming bull:
(A god at play)
Who bears the
Trusting girl away . . .

Listen – the flutes
Are shrill and sweet;
My stones are swished
By dancing feet

Kissing the many-
coloured ring
Of Summer – Autumn –
Winter – Spring . . .

Romans, beware!
Robbers are near!
(The house went up
In flame and fear.)

And now the bull
Could see the sky –
But my mosaic
Stood firm and dry;

So Saxons built
A shed for grain,
And bashed a hole
To sink a drain.

Hop, skip and jump
Let ages pass:
My floor lies dreaming
Under grass

Till children come
On study trips,
Clutching pens
With rainbow tips.

Their teacher won't
Translate my Latin.
"Nobody needs
To copy that in.

Colour your charts
Fill in the blanks."
Dear boys and girls
You owe me thanks:

For I'm the nameless man from Gaul
Whose cunning skill designed it all.

COPPER IN THE MUD

*A more-or-less true tale of not-so-long ago – Gravesend lies
on the River Thames*

Down on the shore by Gravesend Pier
This is the sound that you used to hear:
Dirty girls and boys
All making such a noise
Speaking to the public loud and clear.

"Copper in the mud;   *(quiet – like a spell)*
Copper in the mud;
All we need is a copper in the mud.
Throw one down, sir,
Make it half a crown, sir!
All we need is a copper in the mud."

Plenty of mud – and not a lot of sand:
Up on the pier the passengers stand.
Flat caps - top hats,
"This'll make you stop" hats.
Some a bit scruffy: some very grand.

"Copper in the mud;   *(louder)*
Copper in the mud;
We're down here and waiting in the mud.
We're ever so poor, sir,
Throw one more, sir.
Watch us jump for the money in the mud."

Toffs on the pier have got to pass the time:
Fishing for a farthing can't be a crime.
"Let's make merry
Waiting for the ferry,
Watching the mudlarks splashing in the slime."

Copper in the mud;
Copper in the mud;
Anything you like, but it mustn't be a dud.
"Look at my dress, miss!
O what a mess, miss!
Don't I need a copper in the mud."

Ferry boat's hooting: it's nearly time to go. *(slow)*
See those paddle wheels turning slow.
Mud on your face
Is no disgrace:
So let's get the punters to have another go.

"Copper in the mud, sir?   *(speeding up)*
Copper in the mud, sir?
One more chance for a copper in the mud, sir?
Would you be willing, sir,
To make it a shilling, sir?
Watch me dive for the money in the mud, sir!"

Ferry boat's moving – sending up the spray.
"Gravesend hooligans - better than a play."
"That's not fun, sir! –
Something should be done, sir!"
"Juvenile criminals – lock 'em all away!"

Copper in the mud? Now you may get a lot,
But only if you stand in a suitable spot.
Better not bungle:
Rules of the jungle
Say you-keep-the-loot-you-got.

One posh passenger still doesn't know
That she went and threw a super-silly throw.
Thought it was a copper.
Nobody could stop her.
Gave away gold to the beggars down below.

Treasure in the mud;
Treasure in the mud;
Grab a golden sovereign, gleaming in the mud.
A week's supplies
Of hot meat pies –
And I'll buy everyone a roasted spud.

Copper in the mud;
Copper in the mud;
All we wanted was a copper in the mud.
"I reckon I've won."
"But I got none."
And that's the law of the copper in the mud.

JOHN PASTON'S VALENTINE

The oldest surviving Valentine in English was written by Margery Brews of Norfolk in 1477, and sent to her intended husband, John Paston. Margery was worried that her dowry – 'one hundred pounds and one mark' – would not be enough to satisfy her 'right worshipful and well-beloved Valentine'. *"Wherefore, if ye could be content with that Good, and my poor person, I should be the merriest maiden upon ground . . . and if ye think yourself not so satisfied . . . Good, true and loving Valentine . . . take no such labour upon yourself, as to come more for that matter."*

The dowry was increased; John and Margery were married later in the year.

> Dear Margery Brews,
> How can I refuse
> The offer you graciously make me?
> To ward off distress
> I would like to say "Yes,
> I am yours if you promise to take me."
>
> My merits are small,
> And you are my all.
> I remain your true champion unswerving,
> If our parents agree
> To join you and me
> With a dowry to match your deserving.
>
> One mark and five score
> Silver pounds are far more
> Than my dreams could desire to complete them.
> But the Pastons suggest
> It would be for the best
> If your father rides over to meet them.
>
> On St Valentine's Day
> The birds – so they say –
> Choose mates and prepare for a nest;
> But woman and man
> Must prudently plan
> For bed and for board and the rest.

Farewell for a while!
Remember to smile:
This reply is a true lover's token
That joys shall be free
When our contracts agree:
by JOHN PASTON ESQUIRE, be it spoken!

POSTSCRIPT AND COMMENTARY

by John Coutts, poet and clerk

These verses I found
By digging the ground
Of my mind in a corner marked "MAYBE".
The pair were soon wedded
And boarded and bedded,
And quickly came up with a baby.

Five hundred short years
Have dried the young tears
Of Margery Would-be-a-wife.
More sadly – she cried,
When the little one died,
But was happy for most of her life.

So now I proclaim
The beauty and fame
Of Margery – Valentine Past:
To Valentines Present
We offer this pleasant
Poem – constructed to last.

And could we just say
(It's our *Thought for the Day*)
"Dear Valentines coming to be,
On a basis of trust,
Make love out of lust:
From Margery Brews and from ME."

A LETTER OF THANKS TO LUKE

*Luke dedicated his Gospel – and its sequel, The Acts of the Apostles
– to the 'Most Excellent Theophilus'.
Having received Volume One, his friend replies . . .*

Theophilus to Luke, his friend:
(And now, it seems, his teacher too)
May all the joys you kindly send
Return to you.

I broke the seal, began to read
The scroll, and found my humble name.
A gracious compliment indeed!
But bookish fame

Is ill-deserved. For who would dare
To introduce the startling story
Of One whom you, dear friend, declare
Is Lord of Glory?

Allow me, first, to praise your style:
The Hebrew and Hellenic phrase
In harmony . . . dear Bibliophile,
Your skills amaze!

Herodotus has told of Greeks
Who dared to die for hearth and home,
While stern and earnest Livy speaks
Of warlike Rome,

But you have laboured hard and long
To celebrate a Servant King,
And heard – or heard about – the song
That angels sing.

"Glory to God and peace on earth"
(I quote the anthem back to you).
Greeted that less-than-likely birth.
But will it do?

A desperate man – a weary wife –
A feeding trough to hold the small
Bearer of everlasting life?
And that's not all:

"A sword shall pierce the mother's heart."
(How skilfully your words presage
The end: when truth is torn apart
By hate and rage)

But then, beyond the end, the new
Beginning: one they thought was dead
Makes poor discarded hope come true
In broken bread.

Send me the sequel soon. We know
Our Luke has many tales to tell.
The Best of News has far to go:
And so, farewell.

A STRANGE SHIP ON THE SEASHORE

(A first encounter with the Vikings)

There's a mystery ship on the lonely shore
Where the seabirds cry and the breakers roar.
Come with me:
Let's go and see . . .
Everything's odd:
The hull, the mast, the steering oar,
The prow with the face of an unknown god . . .

They've fixed a flag with an animal's head
High on the beach
Above the reach
Of the tides that slide on the sandy shore.
But is it a bear or a wolf or a boar?
Our king said
"We must find out more:
Don't be afraid:
They've come to trade:
So pray for peace but be ready for war."

Can you see that man with club and shield
Across the bay
Where we used to play,
Climbing the cliff towards our field?
I never saw such a shield before!
Those watchmen look like birds of prey,
Mounting guard on the empty shore . . .

The leader's cloak is green and gold.
Surely you see him standing there
Beside the banner – wolf or bear?
Someone simply has to go
Down that path to the beach below,
To the nameless lord and his ominous crew.
What do they want?
We need to know:
Our king and council have chosen YOU!
Be brave and bold!
Show no fear:
Don't go too near . . .
Just ask them: are you friend or foe?
Off you go . . .

I'll stay here.

THE BAKER'S BOY'S DEFENCE

(an interruption to public worship – first presented in Rochester Cathedral)

The Reader is retelling the the pious legend of the murder of St William of Perth, when The Stranger interrupts:

The Reader: And now, good people, let us hear the story of the Holy Martyr, St William of Perth.

The blessed Martyr William, was born in Scotland, in the city of Perth – in the common language 'St John's Town' . . .

He lived by the art of baking, which he had learnt in childhood. Daily he gave one loaf in every ten to the poor, and daily did the pious believer hear mass in St.Mary's Church. And it came to pass, that on leaving the church, he came upon an abandoned child, wrapped in dirty swaddling clothes. With a heart moved by pity, the blessed William picked up the child, and gave it to a woman to nurse. And as the child grew, he taught him the baker's craft.

Then there came a time when William made a vow to visit the scenes of Our Lord's Passion, taking with him the above-mentioned youth, whom he treated as a son. The servant's name was 'Cokermay Doveni', which in the Scottish tongue means 'David the foundling'. Passing through the kingdom of England they came to the city of Roffa – known in the Saxon language as 'Rochester'.

But when they had been in that city for three days, Satan entered into the heart of that servant. And so, on the third day, after they had left the city on the way to Canterbury, they came to a place where paths divided. Here the deceitful traitor led his master down a byway. Then that base and degenerate pupil seized his opportunity, struck his pious and pilgrim father on the skull, and cut his throat as he lay helpless on the ground . . .

(from *The Golden Legend*)

The Stranger   I claim the right to speak . . .

The Reader   I beg your pardon?

The Stranger   That's the official line –
The stuff you're hearing.
A pious pilgrim dies a brutal death:
A devil-driven villain strikes him down.
That's me.

The Reader   And who are you?

The Stranger   The Baker's baby,
David the foundling, he who did the deed.
Gave you a saint, a shrine, a Festival . . .
Your tale of holy helpless William leaves me
Dumb and defenceless – damned across the ages . . .
I claim the right to cross the gulfs of time
And put my case.

The Reader   You'd better come and do it.

(THE STRANGER COMES FORWARD)

The Stranger   Guilty ! Guilty!
Yes, of course I'm guilty.
I struck the blow. I slew the man. I fled.
I got away with killing. Disappeared . . .
You can't arrest me now. I'm dead and gone
For seven long centuries – a soul adrift
In time's uncertainty and history's falsehood.
I did the deed. I struck my benefactor.
But why?

William, I grant, was honest, pious, gentle...
When people couldn't pay he really did
Give them bread for nothing . . . And he prayed . . .
Just as your story says – and went to church
Just as your story says – and picked me up
Just as it says – and made me Baker's Boy
In Chief . . . and took my gratitude for granted.

Your story doesn't tell you what I felt,
Or what the worthy folk of Perth would tell me:
"David" – they used to say – "You ARE a lucky
Lad – a bastard child whose nasty mother"
(I never knew her name – I still don't know it)
"Dropped her dirty lump of shame and ran.
Just think of that! One day a boy like you –
David, foundling David – could inherit
A bakery, a shop, the lot . . . "
They said my father was a highland robber,
A cattle thief, a filthy mean marauder
Hanged on the Inch at Perth . . .

              The more they said it,
The more I loved the man he might have been.
Hunting the wolf, chasing the restless deer,
Spearing the gleaming, leaping slithering salmon,
Hearing the bard at sundown, harp in hand,
Chanting of ancient kings and glorious quarrels . . .

Those were my happy dreams: but when my foster
Father's baking day was dark and done,
I'd go alone and watch the public gallows
Down on the Inch – the ghastly bodies dangling . . .

So why did William make me wear a badge . . .
Pick up the pilgrim staff and trudge away
To see the Holy Land? – my Land of Freedom
Lay in the north, safe in some fancied glen.
And so at last we came to Rochester –
Dover was next – and after that, the sea.
My time was now or never – seize the money –
Strike like a highlander in Saxon land . . .
And so I struck the blow . . .
I never meant to kill my foster-father;
Only to lay him low and take his money.

"I never meant to kill him" – yes, I know:
Of course they all say that – but still the slit
Throat you heard about is pious fiction.
Is this the truth? Or was your reader right?
Is 'Cockermay' the Scottish word for foundling?
Did I repent? Or did I go on killing?
Your story simply lets me disappear;
And so you'll never know – but please take note:
Out in eternity I face a Judge
Better informed than you.
So put me on your prayer list, kindly people
Who dare affirm the boundless grace of God.
Pray for my soul – and pray for others like me.
Farewell.

(HE DISAPPEARS)

The Reader   After that unexpected interruption to our worship, perhaps it would best if we offered prayer along the lines that our friend has suggested . . .

THE LAST TEMPTATION OF JOHN BUNYAN

(based on Bunyan's own account in 'Grace
abounding to the Chief of Sinners')

John Bunyan didn't have to fret in jail.
He could have stayed at home and mended buckets,
Though King and Parliament had passed a law
To silence fiery Bible-touting preachers,
(Tinkers, they thought, should stick to tinkering)
No one had placed a ban on Bible study
Or private chats concerning moral topics.
Honour the king. Fear God. Go home. Conform.

All this was pointed out by Neighbour Cobb,
A well-intentioned friend. The other options
Were jail, or banishment (Barbados likely)
"Or even worse than that . . . "

As Bunyan sat alone and thought it over
Twenty thousand grinning doubts and devils
Whirled in his mind . . . "My wife, my poor blind child . . .
How will they live?" (for 'worse than that . . .' meant hanging)
Should he give in - and sell his Master? No!
The case against was gospel-clear . . .
                                        . . . unless . . .
Suppose you climb the ladder, noose attached,
Ready to jump – if not, the hangman pushes –
Survey the crowd below you, praying, baying . . .
And then – just then – confront the lurking terror:

"Poor frightened fool, you got it wrong. There's nothing.
No God, no Christ, no crown of life – and now
It's much too late to clamber down again."
This mocking thought, not death itself, was Bunyan's
'Worse than that . . .' - and thus he laid it low:
"Lord, I will clutch my fears" – he prayed – "and then
Leap from the ladder blindfold into eternity:
So catch me if you will, but still, if not
I'll venture for your name."

He didn't die.
He stayed in jail and wrote 'The Pilgrim's Progress'.

CHARLIE DICKENS (JUNIOR) EXPLAINS

He loved his other children best –
Oliver Twist and Little Nell.
I fear we failed the writer's test.
We weren't reviewed. We didn't sell.
He loved his other children best.

Of course Papa deserves his fame.
Just think of Copperfield and Pip
Who magnified the Dickens name
By cab and coach, by train and ship!
Of course Papa deserves his fame . . .

Or Tiny Tim, complete with crutch,
Or simple-hearted suffering Smike . . .
Did we distract him very much?
As heir apparent, I dislike
Poor Tiny Tim, complete with crutch.

By pen and ink and printing press
They stole away the here and now.
We watched our mother's long distress . . .
Dear Pa and Ma, be friends! But how?
By pen and ink and printing press?

At Christmas time he shared the fun.
We played the merry games of Yule
And said "God bless us, every one!"
Dad, was I really such a fool?
At Christmas time he shared the fun.

Oliver dared to ask for more.
We should have shouted: "Let us be!
Papa, you really are a bore.
Immortal author, set us free!"
Oliver dared to ask for more.

WILLIAM BOOTH AT MILE END WASTE

(the beginnings of the Salvation Army, 1865)

When William came at last to Mile End Waste
He saw the grey world sliding to and fro
Like aimless rubbish on the indifferent tide.
And then he heard the dry and evil chuckle
That once beset the Son of Man in person.

"Why waste your time? No saviour died for them.
Bundles of rags redeemed in cheapest gin.
My flock, you know. Poor devils damned already."

Damning despair, he tossed his mane and cried
"Give Lucifer a song – a gospel song."
"Jesus, the name high over all" – at once
The Missioners were bobbing in a mob
Of drunks and drabs and precious souls in torment,
Swarmed from the lurid gas-lit hells around.

"Hurrah" cried William. As the battle brewed
He saw Christ's blood stream in the firmament,
Flaunted before King Satan and his hosts.
Loudly he roared against the assembled fiends
That gripped each pauper by the throat, and perched
On twisted shoulders wrapped in tattered shawls:
" 'Angels and men before him fall' – now, Grandma,
Tell 'em you're saved . . . 'and devils fear and fly.'
Come to the tent at seven. It's warm inside."

Then thudding raindrops washed the crowd away,
And William, plodding through the sodden slum,
Saw Christ's compassion streaming in the gutters,
And dirty cobbles drenched in Holy Ghost.

47

COLLECTING OLD CLOTHES

(West London, 1973)

She packed them in a cardboard box
And locked them in the garden shed:
Neatly folded shirts and socks.
"These were his working boots" she said.
The books, beside his rake and shears
Awaken thoughts too deep for tears.

"His Sunday suit as good as new
Some pensioner might be glad to get . . .
Did you mind me ringing you?
He said he never would forget
Your people's service in the war."
O Time. You blunt the lion's paw.

"Salvation Army'll know a way,
I thought . . . how kind to come so soon . . .
'When I retire' he used to say
'We'll have another honeymoon.'
But then he took his stroke instead . . . "
Have mercy, Lord of quick and dead.

" . . . Leftovers you can use for jumble.
It's lonely really. Folk don't care.
Still, we really mustn't grumble.
Would you kindly say a prayer?"
The rotting shed becomes a shrine;
They also serve who live and pine.

Crowning the carton tied with string
The sacred footwear blocks my view.
Why bother with this sort of thing?
They think you've nothing else to do.
O falsest friend whose base complaint
Profanes the relics of a saint.

COMMUNION OF SAINTS

(Nigeria, 1963)

She lost him years ago, but still
He haunts her, as with loaded head
She carries palm fruit to the mill:
So plainly do the precious dead
Echo her name with gentle breath
Across the sullen stream of death.

Clearest of all her husband calls
Before still morning has begun
To creep within the wattled walls
He built. And here she bore his son:
And here she gravely kneels to pray
For strength to face the blazing day.

And when her tall and learned boy,
Splendid in blazer gold and blue,
Chatters in English – to annoy –
Of foreign things she never knew;
She puts his youthful pride to shame:
And says: "Last night your father came."

"I saw him in my sleep as clear
As though I felt him touch my arm:
What witch – what juju need we fear?
What hooting owl could ever harm?
He keeps us safe who loves us most,
Enfolded in the Holy Ghost."

This quaint and superstitious faith
Psychologists can soon explain:
The dear deceased is just a wraith
Projected from her wishful brain.
And yet she knows that he is there:
Deny it, stranger – if you dare.

DEAD BABY

(Nigeria, 1962)

I heard the triple shriek, and blamed
The nurses in the children's wing.
The hospital should be ashamed;
They ought to stop this sort of thing.

My schoolgirl, clumsy in her plight
Groaned and contorted on the bed.
Why should hysterics have the right
To yell as though to wake the dead?

I turned towards the door, and there
Noticed a little child at rest.
Gracious the dark and curly hair,
The flawless hands on mother's breast.

And yet the woman's eyes were wild;
For very dread she could not weep.
The little one lay calm and mild
Upon her shoulder fast asleep.

We stared, but never knew each other,
And then a white official coat
Appeared before the silent mother:
Clearing a kind and cautious throat

It said – in stilted speech precise,
"Your Mission sir, is much admired.
If you could help, it would be nice.
This woman's baby has expired."

I drove her home, and all the way
She sat bolt upright on the seat.
Curled in her arms the baby lay;
Vainly I struggled to repeat

The immemorial words of peace;
Vocab. and grammar let me down;
Till shame and pity made me cease.
I blew the horn to wake the town.

We left the metalled way; the rain
Danced on the dark and rutted road.
At last the child was home again.
The woman took her tiny load

And stumbled as I held the door.
"Mother, go well", I tried to say,
"God pities you . . . " but as before
Her face was blank. Damp and decay

Assailed us from the bush. She ran
Towards the low and dimlit door.
The child will end where he began
At rest beneath his father's floor.

Now she's at home, and breaks her heart,
Wailing as native women do.
I rev the engine and depart.
Maybe my heart is broken too.

MAD GIRL

From market place to market place
The crazy girl goes round and round
With matted hair and sullen face
The garri[+] scattered on the ground

Is all she eats, and all her drink
Is water from the muddy ditch.
She cannot speak; she cannot think,
She never wears a single stitch,

But like a conscience old and ill
By naughty boys and girls defamed
She haunts the market people still;
Naked she goes; and not ashamed.

Our mechanic told her story
Once when we passed her in the car.
Still in her first ungathered glory
She met a man from Calabar

And proudly said "I'm not for you",
At which the superstitious cad
Put medicine in her rice and stew:
An overdose: it drove her mad.

And so he never had his will,
For sudden terror slew desire.
A week she raved, a month was ill;
Her eyes had lost their youthful fire.

The cruel charm had burnt her brain -
(It cost him several pounds at least)
She never spoke a word again
But wanders like a harmless beast.

I quickly made a mental note,
Testing the car that sunny day,
Of this pre-Freudian anecdote;
Whether it's true I couldn't say.

But many walk on London streets,
Driven by desire untamed
And bruised in heart by life's defeats,
Degraded thus, and stripped and shamed.

* garri is manioc flour: the cheapest food in southern Nigeria

ENCOUNTER

*Many African names are prayer-poems, in which a world of hope
is expressed in two or three words.*

I went to see my friend one day
Between the fields of maize and yam.
It made the children laugh and play
To see my baby in her pram.

How strange her face. How round and red.
(Naked they ran, but not ashamed)
A sweetness soothed my weary head
As one by one their names were named.

"'The-gift-of-God'; my youngest boy"
(Each child stood shyly in his place)
"Next 'Heart-of-Love' and 'Mother's Joy'
'I-see-the-Lord' and 'Fair-of-Face'".

Thus, while the father named them all,
I rested on a bamboo stool.
"This is the eldest one; we call
Him 'George' because he goes to school."

Gravely they greeted me, with grace
Of speech their native tongue adorning,
While George screwed up his learned face,
Coughed, cleared his throat, and said "Good morning".

Three coconuts in homage came,
Borne on a round enamel tray.
I thanked them in my daughter's name,
Loaded the pram and went away:

And still, until we passed the clearing
Where spirits dance beneath the moon,
The children followed, laughing, peering,
Sorry to see her go so soon.

What will become of those who stay –
Well-loved, irregularly fed,
Too soon, alas, shall ringworm lay
Its curse on every comely head.

"Save them from evil, I beseech."
This was my silent parting prayer.
It seemed that thoughts too sad for speech
Hung on the damp oppressive air.

Yet still, as homeward we were going,
My daughter, blotched by sandfly showers,
Gravely observed the women hoeing
And waved her hands at passing flowers.

VOICES FROM THE PAST

WATER BY WEIGHT

(a man's meditation – somewhere in Ghana)

She's got a tin of water on her head.
The old four-gallon can . . . how much in litres?
I wish I'd brought the video camera with me!
Just watch her move: she's like an artist's model . . .
The head held high – and half a mile to go –
Neck long and straight – the shoulders strong and tense -
The coloured wrapper tight about her body;
Blouse half-drenched in sweat and dripping water.
Look out . . .
              She trembles, staggering, muscles taut . . .
Don't drop it, dear . . .

              One naked arm aloft
Steadies the rusty tin. Her feet find ground,
She sways a little, almost like a dancer,
And sails away . . . that tin of hers is leaking . . .
Suppose I went and took a tactful picture?
Made it worth her while, of course . . . Just think:
'THE WATER BEARER, PHOTO WINS AWARD.'
Imagine her enlarged, exposed on countless
Billboards, back in Britain. That should make
The blighters think. Donate the cash, perhaps,
To lay a plastic pipe to reach the village . . .
And then they wouldn't have to carry cans.
She's gone. A bonny sight. Fine woman, fine!
Until the weight of water hurts her spine.

A MODERN PASTORAL

*There seem to be plenty of doom-laden poems about poverty in the
Third World – so I decided to balance 'Water by Weight' with
a modern pastoral in imitation of Theocritus, who wrote about
the shepherds and goat-herds of Sicily long ago . . .*

The incident described in the poem took place in northern Nigeria

"Sister . . . you'll never guess . . . two men, two strangers,
Europeans, whites: I'd never seen them
Quite so close before. I nearly died!
We finished work, I got my load of grain
Carefully balanced, topped with good dry dung -
(Billy-goat does his best) and was it heavy!
Contented bellies cost an aching back!
(Give me a rub!)

       And then I lost the lot!
It all slid off before this pair of MEN,
Strangers, Europeans, holding cameras!
You have to stoop and bend your knees to duck
Under the bridge. I bent a bit too far....
(Just keep on rubbing – thanks!)
       . . . and down it went.

Head-pan, head-pad, hoe, a heap of millet,
Dung, and me . . .oh dear . . .
I piled it up – but now the problem; how
To get it safely on my head again?
Down in the dust I kneel: those fellows come
To crown me, smiling . . .

Here's the joke, dear sister:
The PAIR OF THEM could hardly lift my headpan!
It took two men to load a single woman
And send the humble donkey on her way.
So now we know why foreign fellows ride
In cars . . . and why they're not so good at making
Babies . . . if it's true . . .

(Do keep on rubbing!
My back, my poor old back, my aches and pains!)
Those men with shaky legs and mighty brains
Can always come and go in aeroplanes!"

PROJECT REPORT

(A monologue with dictaphone)

This is a story from Lagos, Nigeria.
The grant came from the charity 'Help the Aged'

"To Projects Office, P.O. Box, etcetera:
Dear Sir, the grant you gave was used as follows:
We purchased thirty plastic bags. In each
We placed a pound of rice, some tea, dried beans,
St. Matthew's gospel in the local language,
Sugar and salt, a box of matches, tinned
Tomato puree, local leaves resembling
Spinach, bananas, oranges, some palm
Oil, and a greeting card."

New paragraph.

"The funds, we trust, were wisely spent: the list
Of aged people checked and double-checked
In case of fraud. The bags were packed on Christmas
Eve, and taken round by volunteers
On Christmas Day. Each team included one
At least who spoke the local language. I
Myself took part . . ."

Old woman, please forgive.

We came to help. I never knew your home
Was bare, so very bare; the walls unpainted
Concrete: never thought we'd scare you stiff,
We strangers bearing gifts. You saw and dreaded
My whitish face and khaki shorts, my thin
Thin lips and pointed nose. Was it police?
Or trouble? Yes – official trouble!

We gave you such a fright on Christmas morning
Attempting to deliver one of thirty
Plastic bags containing . . . never mind . . .

For once you understood, you offered thanks
In long melodious words and solemn gestures
Centuries old. You greeted Khaki Shorts
(Who hardly knows the local language) kindly,
Maternally, a queen beside your charcoal
Fire: then you smiled and made your farewell curtsey
Slowly and gently, being old, but smoothly,
As though the years had spared your maidenhood.
You blessed me then. We went away unsnubbed
And you unpatronised.

       Let's try again:

"To Projects Office, P.O. Box, etcetera:

Dear Sir,
      The grant you gave was used as follows . . . "

WHITE MAN IN AFRICA

If you work abroad, beware of adding local prejudices to the preconceived
ideas you bring with you. Feeling against the Ibo people ran high in non-
Ibo areas before the Nigerian Civil War broke out in 1967.

" . . . So never trust the African, my friend:
That's the first lesson here, and don't forget it.
Believe them, and they'll fool you in the end;
Treat 'em as brothers and you'll soon regret it –
So never trust the African, my friend.

"Corruption's in their blood: they're all infected.
They look like decent chaps in many ways
But do the dirty when it's least expected
And turn and run; and you're the fool who pays.
Corruption's in their blood – they're all infected.

"Ibos are worst of all: just give them rope.
We went and paid them for a drum of fuel –
Gallons had gone; they patched the hole with soap.
That's how they play it here – the country's cruel,
And Ibos worst of all. Just give them rope.

"The country's rotten and the climate's hateful:
The politicians make a song and dance,
(For all we did they're totally ungrateful)
But wretched peasants never get a chance.
The country's rotten and the climate's hateful."

These bitter thoughts are not exactly new.
'Brits are the biggest liars of them all'
Mutters the weary Roman to the new
Recruit who guards the gate on Hadrian's wall.
These bitter thoughts are not exactly new.

An Ibo youngster with an anxious face
Stood on the step, uneasy and expectant.
These were to me the sovereign means of grace:
A badly battered can of disinfectant,
An Ibo youngster with an anxious face.

One of the few whom even I'd believe
He went by truck to see supplies brought in;
A face too frankly honest to deceive . . .
What will he say about that battered tin:
This one in ten whom even I'd believe?

"Sir, I was riding on a Tinker Bus;
I put the stores inside and paid the fare . . .
The passengers piled in and made a fuss,
And suddenly I saw it wasn't there.
You know what happens on a Tinker Bus.

We found the tin a hundred yards away;
The planking in the floor had fallen out -
But when I told the motor boys to pay,
Driver and passengers began to shout:
And so I thought it best to come away.

Chop money doesn't matter sir; you see
 I ate my dinner at my uncle's place."
"Come, come, my son; you fairly earned your fee . . ."
He shakes his head. O brave and honest face.
"Chop money doesn't matter sir; you see . . . "

My trusted friend, my child, my brother now:
Leaving the sacramental tin behind,
Away he scampers, little dreaming how
Mercy through him has drenched a desert mind . . .
My trusted friend, my child, my brother now.

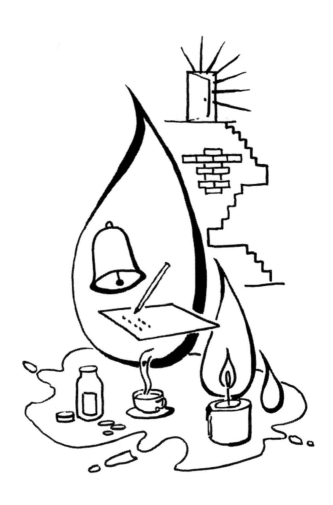

PEOPLE AND PLACES

CARDBOARD CITY

A sponsored poem for Christian Aid Week 1988

Following the introduction of 'Community Care', many old-fashioned Asylums were closed – and the patients found themselves on the streets.

At one o'clock in the morning
The air was mild and damp.
Behind our inquisitive headlights
We found the way to camp.

The site is green and gracious,
The management buildings grand,
With numerous Places of Interest
Conveniently close to hand.

The ground is pleasantly haunted
By England's good and great.
I slid through Oliver Cromwell
Close to the exit gate.

"Watch for Prince Rupert!" I muttered.
"He lies in wait by the pond."
"No problem" said brave Oliver.
"We're pals in the Great Beyond."

But back at the van my leader
Was getting out all the gear.
There was bread in black bin-liners:
I felt a twinge of fear.

The gallant shades of long ago
Provided a camper's treat:
But the ghosts of our glorious present
Were lying on every seat;

Each in a cardboard coffin,
With a leak-proof plastic shroud –
A sample of London's homeless
Sliced from the mighty crowd.

Our job was to offer refreshments:
Soup in a throwaway cup.
My leader said "Ask politely,
It's rude to wake folk up."

I met a crazy lady
Beneath an eerie moon.
"Two soups; two bits of bread, please.
And could you give us a spoon?"

She claims to be having a baby:
I doubt if this is true.
She lies with a Male Companion,
Close to the Public Loo

In a hollow square of cartons,
To keep despair away.
They looked like a couple of hamsters.
The twilit grass was grey.

But these are the Fields of Lincoln's Inn:
It was here, in golden days,
That Master William Shakespeare
Got good ideas for plays.

And still the trees in breathing
Mystery look down,
On homeless Happy Campers
Of timeless London Town.

Back at the van my leader
Said "Yes, my lad, it's tough.
But some of our friends prefer it.
What's wrong with sleeping rough?"

And indeed, the natives were friendly.
They said: please could we stop?
It was hardly Holy Communion,
But I wouldn't call it a flop.

(Except at the Green Pavilion
Where alcoholics lay,
They made uncalled-for comments
Before we drove away.)

At one forty-five in the morning
We left them resting there.
The name of the game, good people
Is modern Community Care.

But still the trees in mercy
And mystery look down
On these, the Hapless Campers
Of booming London Town.

BEWARE OF THE COLLECTOR!

Look who's manoeuvring down our street!
It's Mrs Magnolia, on middle-aged feet.

Carefully coping with every gate
On the even side . . . two . . . four . . . six . . . eight . . .

Heavily armed with faith and hope,
Coming to collect that envelope.

(We aren't keen on her hard labours:
Much too busy watching "Neighbours")

Mrs M. has a stick-on smile.
Mrs Magnolia is full of guile.

"Calling for the envelope – can't you find
It? Here's another one . . . Never mind . . .

Lots of little bits make a lot . . . !"
She took all the change I'd got.

Far away in Somewhere Land
Someone is comforting Somebody's hand.

Close to home, on well-worn legs,
Mrs Magnolia beams and begs.

Far away, in ONE OF THOSE PLACES,
Happiness flickers on sad young faces.

Christian Aid is prowling near:
(We give something every year)

Faraway, in Disaster City
Somebody opens a packet full of pity.

Christian Aid is hovering there,
Helping to show how much we care.

Far away, in a land forsaken,
Water laughs and green things waken.

Back in the Avenue it's getting dark.
Mrs Magnolia avoids the park.

But over the seas in Terrible Town
Someone's fever . . . is . . . going . . . down . . .

As Mrs Magnolia delivers the swag!
Envelopes crammed in a plastic bag.

Now she stumbles, fumbles for a key:
More than time for a cup of tea.

Out on the evens – back on the odd:
"Thank you very much indeed" says God.

SUNDAY SCHOOL TEACHER

What was your Christian name? I can't remember!
Perhaps I never knew: we children called you
Plain 'Miss Furniss'. Was I nine – or ten?
You looked extremely old – but never ugly;
You wore a weekly hat – and never shouted.
Your fingers used to shake a little, holding
The Bible – tiny print in double columns,
Mapless, uncanny, pictureless, and marked
'NOT TO BE TAKEN AWAY.'

                        Your knobbly knuckles
Puzzled me. Why so swollen? Bible lessons
I don't remember much, recalling chiefly
Details about yourself; you finished school
At twelve . . . Can this be right? . . . and plaited straw
For hats. Your pocket money came to tuppence
Weekly. This, divided into ha'pence,
You gave to God in four instalments – once
On Saturdays – and thrice on sacred Sundays.
This WAS impressive! Birthdays came and went:
You used to give us each a slab of solid
Golden toffee, wrapped in thick smooth paper.
Sweets were rationed then . . . I calculated
It must have cost you every single coupon.

Amazing grace! I read my birthday card
Glimpsing mysteries . . . The God you loved
Given so gladly with the broken toffee.
You wished me happiness . . . your fingers trembled . . .

BEYOND WORDS

an Irish dialogue

Dublin: O'Connell Street: a sunny day.
The Irish tricolour is floating free
Above the very spot where Patrick Pearse
Proclaimed the new Republic.

Just for once
I buy the London, not the Irish Times.
The paper man supplies a furtive copy,
Confronts me eye-to-eye, and – what was that? -
Gives me the change in GAELIC: cash correct!
O joy – at last – a genuine Irish speaker
Willing to speak in Irish . . . Then I notice
The wedge of angry papers at his feet.
Those hooded figures holding Armalites . . .
Headline: BRITS OUT . . .

Well, I'm a Scoto-Brit.
I'm here to learn . . . The fellow doesn't even
Know I know a bit of Scottish Gaelic . . .
The great O'Connell stands in silent stone.
The Liffey flows. The traffic stops. The pile
Of bitter print remains unsold.

I go.
But thank you, friend, for greeting me in Gaelic!
I wish I'd had the wit to answer back.

HURRAH FOR MISS HUDSON!
HURRAH FOR MISS HALL!

Hurrah for Miss Hudson! Hurrah for Miss Hall!

Miss Hall was petite and Miss Hudson was tall.
Miss Hall was – well – round . . . and Miss Hudson was thin.
In those days it looked as if Hitler would win.
As brave British soldiers got out of Dunkirk
Miss Hall and Miss Hudson got on with their work -
Though the white cliffs of Dover should crumble and fall.
Hurrah for Miss Hudson! Hurrah for Miss Hall!

Miss Hall had the infants class - year after year.
Her kingdom was kind: her commandments were clear.
We sang "Once two is two – and two twos are four."
And when we had learnt it – we said it some more.
She taught us NEAT WRITING on lines and in squares.
At the end of the lesson, Miss Hall would say prayers.
Just once I was cheeky – but never again!
It was straight to the Head – and he gave me the cane!
I pretended I never felt nuthink at all . . .!
Hurrah for Miss Hudson! Hurrah for Miss Hall!

Miss Hudson made maps with a gelatine glue.
The paper was soggy – the outlines were blue.
Those maps were mysterious – full of odd shapes
Till you wrote in the names of BAYS, RIVERS and CAPES.
On her shelves I discovered some tatty old stories
Extolling Great Britain's Imperial Glories.
Yes! Plenty of Henty – a hoard beyond price!
Gorillas on land: polar bears on the ice.
I explored the wide world though simple and small.
Hurrah for Miss Hudson! Hurrah for Miss Hall!

Adolf Hitler had been – he'd conquered – he'd gone.
Miss Hall and Miss Hudson went on . . . on . . . and on . . .
Each lady quite properly lived on her own
With a cat, and a hot water bottle of stone.
By two in the morning the bottles were cold.
Miss Hall and Miss Hudson would feel rather old.
But they got to school early, come rain or come shine,
Blowing blasts on a whistle to keep us in line.

So . . .
. . .when the world ends, and the galaxies die,
And God rolls away the great scroll of the sky,
(And Christ comes majestic, to gather the lands
With strange and magnificent wounds in his hands,)
Then a voice from High Heaven shall triumphantly call:
Hurrah for Miss Hudson! Hurrah for Miss Hall!

TOP FLAT, TRUEBODY BUILDINGS

Grey stairs go up,
Flight upon flight,
Where huddled flats
Compete for light:

And high above,
Unfree to leave,
Alone, serene,
There dwells Miss Reeve.

The spirit strong,
The heart so frail.
O cruel stairs . . .
Poor breath would fail.

While some men drive
And others drift,
No power on earth
Installed a lift.

Though neighbours call
Each second day,
Truebody Buildings
Holds its prey

Who somehow knows
(Trapped on the landing)
The peace that passes
Understanding.

Her soul is brave,
Her curtains bright.
Miss Reeve inhabits
Realms of light.

To wealthy people's
Girls and boys.
She gave good years:
And now her joys

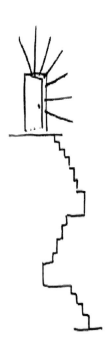

Are these: to share
Fine cake, and show
Old photographs
Before you go.

It's time to leave:
We've done our duty . . .
Stop, fool, perceive
Grace, goodness, beauty!

HE KICKED MY CAR!

in the School staffroom – at coffee break

The villain crossed the street and kicked my car.
It's true. I kid you not. He kicked my car.
He crossed the street and kicked my car on purpose.
I only stopped to buy a loaf of bread:
That's all. The boy was walking home as usual.
No doubt he had a bus-pass once and lost it.
He crossed the street, aimed at my car, and kicked it . . .
With me inside, when I was feeling safe!

(This term, thank God, I haven't even taught him)
Our friend runs true to form, thick as his file.
Of course I know we ought to show compassion . . .
But does he have to take it out on teachers?
We didn't build the Bevin Housing Scheme!
Bad, mad and sad – he terrifies the Head!
Last week it seems he kicked the Social Worker . . .
I've had enough: this time he's gone too far.
Why me? Why pick on me? Why kick my car?

AT THE SHRINE OF ST SERGIUS, ZAGORSK, RUSSIA

November 1988

The candle blessed your youthful face,
Dear friend, whose name I cannot know:
So strangely dark that holy place
Where countless pilgrims come and go.

Yet you and shadowy I have sung
Those anthems far too rich for tears:
On Russian soil to speak the tongue
I waited three and thirty years.

We formed a small impromptu choir:
No names were asked: no strangers barred:
Somebody brought the gentle fire:
You held aloft a home-made card.

The words were blurred, the music dim:
I hid behind a splendid bass
And hummed an old Slavonic hymn,
Glancing sideways at your face

Beneath the painted saints. Join in,
Most Reverend Sergius! Thanks to you
I watched the girl – evading sin –
Amazed by grave believers through

The gloom . . . as one by one they kissed
Your shrine: our candle flickered low.
At last the guide from INTOURIST
Wordlessly whispered "Time to go!"

Dear singing friend whom I shall never
Meet, you gave me grace on grace.
I saw – so briefly yet for ever –
All Holy Russia in your face.

*I learned Russian in the R.A.F. back in the 1950s
but made my first visit to the Soviet Union in 1988.*

*The Monastery of the Trinity was founded by St Sergius
in the 14th century.*

A CHRISTMAS EVE CONFESSION

*at the Church of John the Warrior, in Moscow on January 6th,
1991 – when Christmas was celebrated in public for the first time
since the Russian Revolution*

What are you telling him, solemn and slender,
Scarved in sincerity, shielding your face?
Happy the priest whose attentions are tender . . . !
Is it perplexity, doubt, or disgrace?

Did you let grumbles get out of proportion?
Quarrels in quarters collective run wild?
Climb on the sorry-go-round of abortion?
Shove a poor bàbushka, shout at a child?

What are you whispering, Father-on-duty,
Earnest and urgent, adorning the Word?
Candles and choristers, cunning in beauty,
Hallow your counselling, seen but unheard,

What am I thinking, as worshippers jostle?
Those who see God must be flawless in heart!
Grant me, young woman, unwitting apostle,
Crumbs of contrition before I depart.

Lord of nativity, Light Unexpected,
Down the grey streets muffled Muscovites go.
Hear a poor prayer for that idol neglected:
Lenin impenitent, powdered in snow.

SATURDAY EVENING SERVICE
IN MOSCOW

at the church of the Novodevichy Convent, Moscow, October 1990

Old friend, you took me by surprise.
I felt a sudden twinge of dread.
Your face was oddly still – your eyes
Were shut: you whispered, "Yes . . . I'm dead."

Lying in humble state I found you
Near the shimmering candle-stall:
A boy and girl ran rings around you,
But people didn't mind at all.

At last a bearded bishop came:
They rolled the carpet up behind;
The cantor's voice was roaring flame.
The echoing choir was cool and kind.

Your life I do not dare to guess:
What queues you joined, what floors you polished;
Years of terror. . . . dumb distress;
Churches shuttered, hope demolished;

Stalin's cunning rape of truth –
Adolf Hitler's rude rampaging . . .
Did they snap off your scented youth,
And bruise your slow and painful ageing?

Were you a scamp? A sad disgrace?
A humble bread-and-rouble-winner?
I cannot read your silent face.
Have mercy Lord, on me, a sinner.

And here's the waiting coffin-lid . . .
I wish we had the time to stay . . .
With Christ in God your life is hid:
The people sing your soul away

As I observe the cloud of light
That crowns a larger, noisier shrine:
For Spartak play at home tonight . . .
While Muscovites must stand in line

For salt and sausage, cheese and bread.
The young and echoing choir replies
That Christ is risen from the dead.
Old friend, you took me by surprise.

CHRISTMAS 1947

a boy's encounter with prisoners of war

They tried to sing. It sounded more like groaning.
Each of the prisoners wore a brown or black
Battledress jacket. On the back a patch
Distinguished them from other human beings.
Two were tone-deaf. One – from the Russian front –
Wept when a toddler smiled at him . . . but why?

How could I hate – deriving biased views
Of Adolf Hitler from the Beano comic?
Mine was a lovely war. The nearest buzz-bomb
Landed in Bricket Wood a mile away . . .
It took a day of summer butterflies
To find the crater.

           When they shuffled in
I tried my first-year German out, but theirs
Differed. They stood in line: an awkward squad
In church if not in war. The preacher smiled.
They sang – or groaned – so slowly, sadly, slowly . . .
Whoever heard a noise like that before?
And then a second verse! Before the end
I recognised the tune – which was – amazing –
My far-from-favourite carol: 'Silent Night'.
When it was over, everybody clapped.
How very odd: odd as the Word Made Flesh . . .

THE SCAVENGER'S TALE

somewhere in the Third World

I've got a job collecting tins
From gutters, dumps and rubbish bins.

The days are long, the profits poor:
Nobody dares to ask for more.

If tins are scarce I hunt for rags
Or poke around for plastic bags.

Before we start I always pray:
"Good God, do give me glass today."

You foreign friends may think it funny:
To me a crop of these means money.

An airtight jar! – The lid screws down
They buy them up in HardshipTown

To store their coffee, salt and tea:
The deal will make a meal for me.

If greedy ants invade your street
Searching for sticky things to eat

Stay calm. Remember you can hide
Your stock of sugar safe inside.

Your trash . . .
         . . . my cash.

ON THE THE SOUP RUN

George Square, Glasgow

We did not bring a lot:
Soup in a plastic cup,
Tasty and thick and hot.
Shaking, you drank it up.
We sniffed the winter air
That evening in the Square.

We also had some bread
Donated by a store.
"That's grand, that's grand," you said
And seemed to want some more;
Which we were glad to share
That evening in the Square.

So were you sleeping out?
You quickly answered: "No".
This we took leave to doubt.
But had to let it go.
Tourists began to stare
That evening in the Square.

We brought no cup of wine
Blessed by the Son of Man.
Making no sacred sign
We loaded up the van;
But surely He was there
That evening in the Square.

THE PEANUT SELLER

an encounter with debt bondage

I'm the cheeky peanut seller,
Everybody's favourite fella.

Meet me in the motor park
Any time from dawn till dark.

Here's another loaded truck,
Watch me try my trader's luck.

"Tasty peanuts, best in town!"
No one knocks my prices down.

I'm in business – no one's fool:
Don't have time to go to school.

Every single cent I get
Goes to clear my mother's debt.

Sorry, pal – no time to play.
Still . . . I'll strike it rich one day.

I'm the cheeky peanut seller,
Everybody's favourite fella.

Any time from dawn till dark
Meet me in the motor park.

IN MEMORY OF A NIGERIAN BOY

He never came for interview
Although I gladly changed the date.
We sent a message by canoe:
It came too late.

After the test he spent some weeks
In working at the fishing camp
Among the far unnumbered creeks,
Deadly and damp.

His elder brother – now class five –
Brought me his photo for the file.
I never saw the lad alive
And now his smile

Recalls the old uneasy sorrow
Of daffodils too soon departing,
Of eager hopes with no tomorrow,
Old memories smarting.

Yet here, where children often die,
No tender metaphors avail.
All night the drums complain and cry,
The women wail.

His mother, through the storm of grief,
Could hear his restless spirit call.
Well she confessed her dread belief
And cursed them all.

She cursed the other wives by rote:
She cursed the children one by one;
Fearful the curse with which she smote
The second son.

Foul play, she cried, had done the deed.
(The village shook in wild alarm)
What else could make his bowels bleed
But some dark charm? –

Too evil for the light of noon
But hallowed to the work of hate
By mumbled charms beneath the moon,
Stronger than fate,

Stronger than Him of whom she hears,
Still in her floral Sunday best.
No Son of Man can dry her tears,
Ease her unrest.

Now to placate her murdered son
She calls the powers of stone and spring
To wreak dread vengeance on the one
Who did this thing.

Duly he sickened, nearly died,
Duly confessed he had a charm.
It cost him forty pounds, he cried,
He meant no harm.

The eldest brother sent to school
To ask my learned colleague's aid.
I let him go – against the rule –
And so he stayed

A day at home to patch up peace
(I had to lend my cycle too).
Slowly his mother's furies cease,
The sun shines through.

The second son regains his health;
Our lad returns to Lit. and Trig.,
My syllabus (the Commonwealth)
Is rather big;

And so relentless duties drive
Poor feckless pity from my mind.
The face I never saw alive,
So young and kind,

Startles me now; I hesitate
Before I cross him off the list.
No whinings from this candidate
At chances missed.

Quietly I sit: I know another
Has dried his tears and cooled his brow.
One who still searches for his mother
Accepts him now.

ELEGY FOR THE THIRD COOK AT AKAI SECONDARY SCHOOL, NIGERIA

Isaiah died the other day;
One of a large and sickly brood,
He earned the usual monthly pay
Of one pound seven and six plus food.

The boys approved his cooking though.
They liked the way the soup was blended.
He put the pepper in just so.
Now his creative work is ended.

He only stayed a little while;
Just recently I learnt his name.
So young he met the fiery trial:
So swift the gastric torture came.

He sent a lad to deputise
Through one slow crawling week of dread;
I heard the news with some surprise.
Before I saw him, he was dead.

The end of term wound up his pain
The boys who loved him gasped with fright,
Waylaid me in the driving rain
And said they wouldn't stay a night.

Their anxious spokesman tracked me down,
Wrapped in a blanket like a shroud.
So frank a face disdained to frown
At my reproaches long and loud.

"We know you won't be pleased at all
To let him go, but who would dare
To sleep so near the dining hall
Now that Isaiah's ghost is there?"

Part Two

To own its all too frequent dead
The village clusters at the door.
Portions of Job are duly read
Over the coffin on the floor.

In this squat house of thatch and clay
The boy was born, and here he died.
Under these eaves he learnt to play;
At first and last his mother cried.

Brief joys she had, but sweet indeed:
As when he scampered home from school
To show the book she cannot read.
Now death has made her look a fool.

Half naked on the floor she lies:
I mumble some dull phrase or other.
Blank are the bleared unseeing eyes
That prove her every inch a mother.

Then, turning from that stricken stare
I hurry down the sandy lane.
To one small plot the boy was heir,
Into his own he comes again.

Beside a pit scooped out of mud
The hurried coffin soon arrives.
The bearers chant of Jesus' blood;
The ruthless vegetation thrives.

Filled to the brim with good intentions,
Longing to ease the heart's sore strife,
The brash young preacher briefly mentions
The Resurrection and the Life.

And I, perspiring, strange and white,
Struggle to share the common grief;
Instead, as insects hum and bite
I own my secret unbelief

And watch the mourners shovel earth,
The men who stamp inside the grave –
Was it for this she gave him birth?
And does he have a soul to save?

I turn and take a final look,
Almost too bothered to regret him;
The school will need another cook . . .
The boys no doubt will soon forget him . . .

Yet though through weary weeks I cry
That perfect love should conquer fear
Their ancient terrors make reply:
They know his ghost is brooding near

Lost in the dark where day by day
Ancestral generations sank.
Triumphant on their nameless clay
The unrelenting bush grows rank.

Accept, O Lord, Thy stricken son,
And if Thou never let'st him sink,
Thy love, that moves the stars and sun
Is stronger than I dare to think.

TEENAGER IN TEARS

I swear we met by accident
Where overflowing dustbins keep
Unchanging guard. I never meant
To watch you weep.

Where walls of blankest brick depress
Beside the fence of rotting wood,
There I surprised your young distress;
How strong and good

You are: for when we cleaned the club
And mentioned work – unpaid – to do,
Which of the gang turned up to scrub?
No one but you.

So scorn to him who takes in vain
Bright hair, red eyes, and glistening tears,
Mocking the passion and the pain
Of fourteen years.

The club is packed, the mob enjoy
Hubbub and heat: the records blare.
He drinks a coke - that virgin boy -
Quite unaware

How you – who fled in floods of tears –
A woman scorned, a child distressed,
Baffled by new desires and fears
Of womb and breast –

Bumped into me. That Greek who spied
A maiden goddess in the nude
Was chewed by dogs, I think, and died:
Forgive your rude

Poet, my girl; when cruel time
Brings harsher tears, recall how true
A grace I glimpsed and set in rhyme:
Pure naked you.

LEPROSY PATIENT

I'm glad you came: there's jubilation
On every graduation day.
Of course, we share the celebration
Although we stay.

Each leper cleansed receives a letter;
Also a card from all the staff.
You'll see them dance to prove they're better;
You'll hear them laugh.

Me? You could say I missed the bus.
The doctor gave me quite a shock.
Sentenced to life, it seems: why fuss?
I have a flock

To tend, a field to hoe. The child
You rescued from a forest cage —
Remember? — scratching, biting, wild:
We fixed his age

At ten — you wouldn't know he's ill.
The box of paints your wife's kind heart
Provided soon unearthed a skill,
He's learning art.

Oh yes: the girl you both brought in
Remember how she cried and cried?
The patch has gone, and left her skin
Fit for a bride.

She goes this week – to face a fate
Worse than death perhaps: for frightened
Lads avoid the leper's curse.
Our unenlightened

Countrymen can cause us grief,
But still, the High Life Band will play
For dance and prayer. A First Class Chief
Will grace our day.

And we've got your canoe. I'll admit it was pleasant
To watch it take shape from heart of the tree.
And I dare you to make the traditional present:
A gourd of palm wine to the god of the sea.

My hands let me down, so I chisel no more,
And I miss the long paddle across the lagoon,
And the smell of the nets as they dry on the shore,
And fisherman singing to charm the old moon.

We carved her in love, so I think that you'll find her
Steady . . . That's right, here they come! The Town Mummers
You British would call them . . . a leper designed her,
Your boat . . . Dear oh dear, I must deal with those drummers!

Goodbye. Don't take my words amiss.
I'm glad you've come. Extremely glad.
On jubilation days like this
Who dares feel sad?

"BLESSED ARE THE PEACEMAKERS"

a story from the Nigerian Civil war

I found him writing letters to the Pope
Pleading for peace; he also corresponded
With civic dignitaries and heads of state,
And when the British Council expert mentioned
That Africans are prone to mental illness
("A sudden stress triggers it off") he simply
Smiled and hoped the Pope would intervene.
The British Council man requested me
To visit when we both got back to Lagos.

No-one can claim he wasn't offered treatment.
At home the juju doctor cut a white
Cockerel's throat on his behalf and poured
A calabash of wine. Meanwhile, in contrast,
They tried electric shocks at Tooting Bec.
The clergy rallied round: a young policeman
Stopped him falling underneath a bus,
Remarking, "Steady, Sunshine, take it steady:
We can't afford to lose a future barrister,"
I too devoted precious time, attempting
Counselling – non-directive, non-judgemental –
And still maintain maternal deprivation
Explains the case, plus, naturally, the massacres
To act as trigger. He proposed a conference
Called by U Thant, to care for refugees
And stop the strife. United Nations Troops
Should man a buffer zone. I smiled and listened.

Of course, the lad was plainly schizophrenic.
The troops at Lagos airport picked him up
Prattling of peace. He planned to pray with leaders
On either side. Festooned with ammunition
The redcaps rushed to the asylum. Sirens
Wailed – but once they got his trousers down
A needle in the buttock stopped his nonsense.

The day before Biafra broke away
I found him: dressed in striped pyjamas. Sadly
He asked for paper to inform the Pope.

A fortnight later came the shooting war,
Nigerian troops – the Federal First Division -
Ousted the rebels from the town of Gakem.
I sat beside him on the backless bench
Reserved for visitors. We wondered when
The war would reach his home. His eyes rolled upward
His fingers twitched. The rediffusion system
Blared an inspiring tune. The latest news
Followed. A crackling voice cried "Liberation".
Of course. "United Nations Force" he mumbled.

They smiled, and brought him yet another pill.

SMALL SON

My little son, at ten months old,
Daily aspires towards the stars.
Tired of his cot, awake and bold,
He stands and shakes the trembling bars;

What brave new worlds to win today?
He sees his bleary dad and grins.
Adventure calls: up and away.
Too young to tell mistakes from sins,

He loves to drop his bread and jam,
Considers puddles wholesome fun:
He scowls at strangers from his pram
And loves the text: "My will be done".

Through Kierkegaard is not for him
He shrinks away in shuddering fear
To see the great umbrella grim
Filling the sky and moving near.

He's learnt a lot, my little boy,
Since first I saw him months ago.
From total grief to total joy
He keeps on crawling to and fro.

And grief will often come again:
Greater grief than bumps on head –
The weary weight of mental pain
That leaves the exhausted spirit dead.

Now, for my young, uncertain son
I pray, that as by elders shown,
He learns what duties must be done,
What vices strictly left alone,

May nothing foul his spirit sear,
Or drive his youthful longings under;
May his bright eye be ever clear,
Filled to the brim with sudden wonder.

Still water gleaming in a pail
He contemplates with wild surmise.
May that amazement never fail,
Nor dull despair besmear his eyes,

But evermore, before his fist,
May gracious blossoms bloom and sway,
As by the brooding spirit kissed
In Eden on the primal day.

SEARCHING FOR THE SITE OF
SHAKESPEARE'S THEATRE

This is the site. At least I think it is.
Grass grew here once. The Thames ran wide and shallow.
Some disadvantages were felt in winter
When jewelled gentlemen who came by boat
Squelched ankle deep in mud. The rain, he said,
It raineth every day on king and clown.

But when young summer sparkled on the living
Stream – oh then the banner fluttered bravely
Above the Globe. The trumpeter gave tongue,
The boatmen skimmed like insects on the water,
The manyheaded mob came clutching pennies,
The gaudy Prologue cried his lines, and over
In Fish Street – kind and godly mothers worried.

Here, as young Juliet died for Romeo,
Sad sighing filled the thatched theatre, sited
Midway between the Bearpit and the brothels.

As Portia spoke of mercy unconstrained,
Some crooked streets away, on London Bridge
Severed heads askew among the pigeons
Mocked at her message. Now the asphalt road
Buzzes with cars. The Thames is cased in concrete;
This grubby warehouse even lacks a window.
Where Shakespeare stopped, feeling another play
Stir in his restless brain, a red-eyed vagrant
– Unroyal Lear, three centuries adrift –
Stumbles and drops his bottle. As it shatters
He stands and curses everything and nothing.

THE HAZEL WHITE HOUSEWARMING POEM

(first recited on behalf of the Medway Little Theatre at the Cloister House, the Precinct, Rochester, on November 29th, 1997)

Hazel White
Takes to flight,
Leaves her home of long delight.

Now the cloister
Proves her oyster:
Heavenward let the clergy hoist her.

Dean and Chapter
Think they've trapped her.
"Caught a packet" would be apter.

Our Theatre
– Still her debtor –
Wishes happy days and better.

Helpful Will
Shakespeare still
Whispers: "Act and read and your fill.

Plots shall thicken
Paces quicken:
Evil from the text be stricken."

Hazel, move!
Jump that groove:
What a lot you have to prove.

Here let grace
And fun embrace:
Flowers of joy shall fill this place.

YOUNG VOICES

(but can you hear them?)

"It's cold, it's wet, it's getting dark.
They've shut the shops and locked the park.
Back home was hell. I ran away.
I wish I had a place to stay."

"They told me I was born to fail.
I talk real tough. I'm scared of jail.
They bang you up. It isn't fun.
I badly need a break. Just one."

"My mind's OK. My thoughts are clear.
I try to speak. But can you hear?
I may look scary, strange and slow.
But why not smile and say hello?"

"A stranger put me on a plane,
But will I see my mum again?
This is a weird and wealthy land -
Please, people, try to understand . . ."

HE CANNAE READ!

He cannae read!
I catch a glimpse of teenage Jack:
He sits bewildered at the back.
He does exactly what he's told,
Wears a school tie of red and gold . . .
I'll start again: more haste – less speed!
But he cannae read!

He cannae read!
I write it up: he takes it down.
His fist is clenched: he wears a frown.
His pencil breaks. I lend him mine.
The work is done: his book looks fine.
"But sir" – he says – those eyes do plead!
"I cannae read!"

He cannae read!
It's true: the words don't mean a thing.
"I'm glad you told me: why not sing . . .
Or draw . . . or act . . . record a tape?"
The bell says stop. The boys escape:
And if at first you don't succeed . . .
But he cannae read . . .

FOR ALL THE SAINTS

celebrating 'May's Mission' – later the Salvation Army Hall,
Denton, Gravesend

If stones could praise
And bricks could pray,
They'd thank the Lord
For William May;

The Mission Man
Who ran the show
In hungry years
Of Long Ago;

With Band of Hope,
And Boys Brigade,
And Christ in glory
On parade:

Plus Bible Women
Strong in text,
By noisy children
Unperplexed –

Or driven daft
By urchins' tricks?
Just ask the silent
Stones and bricks

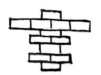

Retained in God's
Thick files of grace,
When Mrs.Clayton
Ruled the place:

– A strong Salvation
Citadel,
Whose kitchen sink
Had tales to tell

Through slump and blitz . . .
But Gospel Praise
Is less in vogue
In doubting days

And Sister Duty
Seems uncool;
Yet still we play
The holy fool,

And join today
In love and laughter
To say "well done"
To brick and rafter,

And start the game
Of grace again –
World without end.
Hurrah! Amen.

with thanks to Gravesend Historical Society

MALADJUSTED BOY

Children who feel secure are good as gold:
(So says the latest influential book)
But watch with care the grinning seven-year-old
Who found his brother hanging on a hook.

The scar along the temple hardly shows –
If only skin and bone were all that mattered!
So quickly youthful tissue heals and grows
You'd never guess how badly he was battered.

But wounded minds, of course, take quite a while:
Misjudgements may occur. In case of error
Record it in the confidential file:
That one may smile and smile, and be a terror.

"Steady, my son. Of course it's interesting
To play policeman. Super fun to try out
The plastic helmet. Fancy, you're arresting
Poor harmless me. You ass, you'll put my eye out!

It's sharp – that broken torch. Say after me:
'Sharp, sharp' – dear dear, your mouth is stuffed with toffee!
Bad boy to poke it in my face, you see,
O when will teacher finish having coffee?

Back to your page of sums. Now aren't you clever!
You've got them right. I like a boy who tries."
A tick from me – a smile from you . . . oh never
Shall I forget those young and wounded eyes!

"Play the recorder? Splendid! I can teach
A tune or two. Good lad, you try as well.
Finger and thumb like this . . . don't puff and screech!
You make it sound like suffering souls in hell."

Here's teacher back at last. She'll help you grow
In faith and hope. Or should I say: relate
In depth to people? Child, I'd like to know
Whether your parting smile is love or hate.

"I SAW THE BOY WHO SHOT ME..."

(after the Nigerian civil war)

"I saw the boy who shot me"
– My former pupil said –
"The very one who got me!
He did his best to pot me
And smashed my arm instead.

He fought to save Nigeria.
I – for Biafra bled,
Deep in the dark interior,
By cunning state hysteria
And propaganda led.

The Dutch Red Cross descended
And flew me off to bed.
My shattered elbow mended;
My jungle warfare ended:
But not the dreams of dread.

The kindly Dutch allot me
Good books and daily bread:
But still – he really got me,
The nameless boy who shot me:
He'll watch me till I'm dead."

GUY FAWKES DAY

Your hat is falling off
Poor persecuted Guy.
Although you seemed a toff
Enthroned on high,

You topple down to hell –
It's burning now, not hanging –
As timid spirits yell
At fireworks banging.

Soon we shall celebrate
With hot potatoes roasted
Your just tho' dreadful fate.
In vain you boasted

That you could overthrow
King, Council, Palace,
Hundreds of years ago.
We bear no malice,

But ritually remember
Your brave and cruel blunder,
Which fills, this chill November,
Young eyes with wonder.

Dear boys and girls, poor Guy,
Absolved by clearest laughter,
Leaves to the spangled sky
Cold ashes after.

So celebrate the mystery,
Enjoy the hallowed game,
While I, oppressed by history
See flesh in flame.

WRITER IN PRISON

Why me? When all I did was write a book?
Not even that – it isn't finished yet!
What gain or glory does the author get?
Complete seclusion in a concrete nook!
So – People's President – it seems I shook
Your palace battlements! You WILL regret
Arresting me: just now – I'm in the net,
But you're the one who can't get off the hook.

Wait till I autograph the millionth copy
Of 'Satires on the State' by Mr Me!
Lone writer dares to shake a tyrant's throne.
Just watch it – government – I'm getting stroppy!
You'll soon be laughing stocks – just wait and see!
 . . . It's hours to feeding time. I'm all alone.

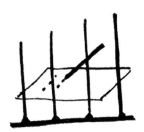

PARADISE LOST

The record she played – when the mob had departed –
Was Harry the Heart-throb, the Lord of All Song:
And she told me – yes, me: unconverted, hard-hearted –
How she queued for his concert one summer night long.

How she and her Best Friend had waited and waited
In jungles of Hammersmith – just for a look.
O moment of ecstasy, fleeting and fated,
When the troubadour wrote in her autograph book!

What singer so gentle, so good, so appealing?
She bought a bright poster and stood on her bed
And fixed Heart-throb Harry with care to the ceiling.
"So now – he can watch me undressing!" she said.

Last week, at her gate, unaware of the risk –
Indeed, it was only a quarter to ten –
While deliciously dreaming of Harry's new disc,
She discovered – the hard way – some facts about men.

She was gallant and young: as the foe fell upon her
She struggled and screamed till the villain escaped
From a man on a moped – who acted with honour . . .
So that only her mind – and the bushes - were raped.

Now she lies on her bed and looks up at the ceiling:
She doesn't undress . . . or request the new song.
And poor paper Harry won't know what she's feeling:
Unweeping, unsleeping, the winter night long.

Of course, she is young . . . and her life lies before her . . .
Most men are quite decent . . . and sharp sudden frost
Never lingers in May . . . but what can restore her
The joy of those records, that Paradise Lost?

THE DEAD CHILD SPEAKS A SPELL
FROM THE SPIRIT WORLD

in support of an International Non-governmental Organisation

My mother bought a leather charm
And bound it tightly round my arm:
I cried and coughed and coughed and cried
To sound a small and sad alarm.

My anxious mother bravely tied
Me on her back and hitched a ride
To reach the clinic far away.
Those busy Sisters really tried

To hold me tight and make me stay,
But soon I slept – and slipped away.
The Spirit World is O-so-near.
Go gladly, strangers, as you pay

That hasty tribute once a year
To banish dirt, disease and fear.
I am beyond all hate and harm,
So spare a thought, a prayer, a tear . . .

SENDING ISAAC HOME

*In many third world countries, children pay fees to attend school
and have to leave if they do not pass the annual examinations.*

"Please sir, I hear reports are out."
"Yes, Isaac, in the post."
"But my result, sir?" Now the uneasy doubt . . .
Granted his marks were even worse than most . . .
Staff meeting had agreed the boy must go:
But could they see that dark and anxious face,
Mask of a mind bewildered, young and slow,
Those silent eyes, pleading for grace . . .

I briefly hesitate: there's no solution,
On with the slow and brutal execution.
"I'm sorry, son, you haven't found it easy,
And education isn't all, you know . . ."
Stop trying to be breezy!
Tell him the truth and let him go!
"You've failed again, my boy, and by the rule,
We can't allow you to return to school."

A thousand years of silence seem to follow.
The unrelenting sun still burns;
The palm trees stand in dark secretive clumps,
A vulture flops among the rubbish dumps,
And I affect a patience sick and hollow.
"Come, Isaac, take it like a man!" He turns,
My office seems a grim and hostile land –
"Please, sir, I do not understand."

"You've failed. The mark sheet's here for you to read.
I wrote to Lagos to inform your brother."

Now his Gethsemane begins indeed,
Disquieting me with glimpses of Another
Who waited silently for condemnation,
Judging the twisted face of greed.
As I, great Caiaphas, all pity smother,
Slowly he reels beneath my blow;
And half a lie is all my consolation:
It's better for the school that one should go.

One further question from the jaws of hell:
"Please, sir, excuse me, can you tell
My mark in English?" On his ruin bent
I thrust him to the pit: "Sixteen percent!"
Denying him one kindly lie
So brutally his dreams I crucify.
He takes the stroke without a sound
And in his trembling mouth no guile is found.

How old he looks, there on the football field
Where once he daydreamed of the first eleven.
        Forever lost his heaven,
The hopes a School Certificate would yield;
        Where glory streams from far
        With comfort, cash and car.

Back to the hut bedraggled by the rain,
The battle with the bush, day after day,
Grubbing for yams down in the shapeless clay.
        So stricken Isaac mourns,
        Nursing his secret pain;
His bright school cap a mocking crown of thorns!
And yet, for all the sour in heart may say,
I know for lads like him the Lamb was slain.

ON THE WAY TO THE CLINIC

The Ethiopian mother's Good Friday Prayer

Lord of the aching, the haze and the heat,
Lord of the pathway that bruises my feet,
Here is my little one, silent and thin,
Tied to my back, very close to my skin.

Lord of dry lips and the struggle for breath,
Let her not slip to the slumber of death.
O how I wish we could rest in the shade!
Better not stop – I'm alone and afraid.

Why is my daughter so feeble and ill?
Is there a clinic just over the hill?
Jesus, I know they were cruel to you!
Let there be doctors who know what to do.

Lord, on Good Friday you went all the way:
Give me the strength to keep going, I pray!
Lord of the cross, you gave all you could give!
Help us to get to the clinic – and live!

STARTING AGAIN

A door has closed,
So leave behind
Rage and regret
That twist the mind.

You stand before
Tomorrow's day.
Open the door
To find a way.

You cannot know,
And dare not guess.
'Will be' and 'was'
Are yours to bless,

So join with friends
And risk a vow
To live in God's
Eternal Now.

IN MEMORY OF SAMIR IBRAHIM SALMAN

bellringer at the Church of the Nativity in Bethlehem

shot on April 5th, 2002

He loved to climb the tower and clang the bell
In Bethlehem, where Jesus Christ was born.
Chimes for the times: he knew them O-so-well . . .
He tried to ring again on mayhem morn.

The cave (or manger site) is down below,
Where pilgrims kneel to pray their pious fill.
Our bellman climbed the stairs. He didn't know
The hour had come to kill and counter-kill.

Samir was just a simple soul, of course . . .
The wary watching sniper held his breath
And put his trust in skilled and deadly force.
A shot ran out. The bellman bled to death.

Christ in the crib, he rang the bells for you.
Forgive. We gunmen know not what we do.

A BUNCH OF VALENTINES

FOR A DEAR ONE LOST
IN A GREAT CITY

The city hurries by tonight,
And harsh and heavy is her breath.
Drenched in a sick and yellow light
She totters to an aimless death;

And in the park the falling leaves
Conceal the rubbish of the week.
Above the lake a seagull grieves;
The clouded moon is blear and bleak.

Yet far away the stealthy tide
Covers the mud of human strife,
The seasons and the sea abide
In rhythms of eternal life.

And now I see my dear one's face,
True as the silent stars are true.
She bathes her naked soul in grace
As weary flowers are bathed in dew.

113

A VALENTINE

first love remembered

I thought the grass would understand.
Leaves of the elm by which we stood –
As crinkled as a baby's hand –
Proclaimed our strange transaction good.

Those dark and aged oaks – were they,
Like you, instinctively aware
Of all I had to say and do
Although till then I didn't dare?

We reached the trees and turned about
And only then the spell was broken.
I sensed the minutes running out,
For all was felt and nothing spoken.

They gonged the gong – and then I knew
The time was either now or never.
"I think I'm sort of fond of you"
I said. Odd line – to last for ever!

You have recalled what I forgot.
The moving shapes of cloud on sky,
The swings – were they in use or not? –
The maladjustment of my tie.

I think you never said a word.
I only dared the lightest kiss.
We seemed at one with darting bird
And moving air. Remember this:

In that strange moment all began.
Desire was felt in finger-tips
And hurried breath. Long-lonely man
Did not aspire to eyes or lips,

But, unrejected, growing bolder,
Shyly possessed you with an arm
So lightly placed on neck and shoulder
As though to shield a child from harm.

Nor could we know – enchanted we,
Not yet entrapped in time again –
That those who set each other free
Must share the load of mental pain.

Next day I said I'd write: the bus
Appeared too soon. We had to part.
Not long! Young lovers, learn from us
The spirit's game, the body's art.

A VALENTINE IN BEREAVEMENT

I saw you give another kind of love,
Dear friend, so skilled in one, so apt in all.
I watched you, thoughtful, calm and undismayed
Before the silent mystery of death;
Listening, smiling, touching, speaking, playing
A subtle counterpoint of true compassion.
O this was finest soul-and-body business,
This comforting of yours, this reckless kindness:
Spending your strength to bless the one who grieved.
I bless you now, exhausted, wan, bereaved.

VALID FOR EVER

Long ago it was BALHAM I chose for my dwelling
And came to my love on the underground train.
But sometimes I cycled at speeds beyond telling
Through London to Euston and homeward again.

Beneath me the Northern Line rumbled and tarried.
Clapham South, Clapham North . . . clatterbang . . . Waterloo:
"How many long months till at last we get married?"
I gasped – racing onwards to exquisite you.

To BARKING by taxi one day I proceeded,
And there at long last my dear girl became mine.
A ring and a prayer and a promise were needed:
We left by the old METROPOLITAN line.

From St Pancras to Scotland by train matrimonial -
I recall, from the days of pure pleasure and steam,
A morning of moorland, grey ramparts baronial,
A truth beyond telling, a joy beyond dream.

Then overground, underground, far we have wandered
By airline and sea-lane, by dug-out and bus:
How often, my dear, have I wondered and pondered:
Who brewed the enchantment that unified us?

No matter, ST VALENTINE, this affidavit
I call you to witness: in spite of spent youth,
My love is as valid as when I first gave it,
For travel together in limitless truth.

VALENTINE FROM A HOSPITAL WARD

(Hawick Cottage Hospital, February 1980)

The landscape is cold, and the robin knows hunger.
The ward is as warm as the African sea:
I recall how we swam there together when younger:
The orderly brings me a cup of weak tea.

The rugby was cancelled: King Wintertime covers
New mud and old grass in an ocean of snow.
Beyond the tall goal-posts – too young to be lovers –
A pair of explorers in Wellingtons go.

The river runs dark, with grey ice at the edges:
A sackful of nuts has been hung for the birds.
The robin disconsolate hops upon ledges.
The blue-tit takes all . . . as I battle with words . . .

Last night it was cold in that house beyond heating:
Adrift in my blankets I dreamt about you:
Let surgery triumph in middle-aged meeting:
With me reconditioned – repaired – nearly new.

For when He of the Face Mask leaned over my trolley
And gave the injection that ushered me out,
I knew for a fact that true love is no folly:
But stronger than frost – and far deeper than doubt.

A SPELL FOR VALENTINE'S EVE

No one in the house but me!
(Plus the clock that mocks and ticks)
Let me sit, alone and free,
Till the bubbling kettle clicks,
Calls me forth to make the tea.

Feel the stillness – let it last!
Taste the hot and sticky brew!
Motor bikes, rat-tatting past,
Stun my solemn thoughts of you.
Write the poem slick and fast.

Boys will soon be back from play:
Time promotes them all to men.
We – who still command the day –
Shall we feel our spring again
When the birds have flown away?

Tell the truth we surely know:
Cast the spell, renew the vow.
Perfect love lays anguish low,
Let our joys be here and now.
Speak the poem . . . clear . . . and slow.

STAGES

The love you gave at first was shy,
Your face was young; your eyes were kind.
You little knew my naked mind;
We lay and watched a gentle sky.

But soon desire grew bold and strong,
Fierce at fulfilment long delayed.
We wrote, we lay apart, we prayed . . .
The weeks, the months, the years were long.

At last our common love was warm,
Close as the equatorial night,
When insects danced around our light,
To die before the hissing storm . . .

We soldiered on . . . to self-despair,
When all we did was done in vain,
(Misunderstanding, mutual pain
And poor dumb loyalty were there)

And came at last to self-disgust:
The body bruised, the flesh despised . . .
In tears and reckless truth surprised,
We learned to speak, to hope, to trust.

So now the love we share is kind,
And clear and calm and cool and deep.
Join hands, and drift away to sleep,
Fulfilled in flesh, assured in mind.

A VALENTINE: THONG LANE, GRAVESEND

I watch you walking slowly up the hill:
Fields to the right and houses to the left:
The Thames beyond, an arc of gleaming grey.
I check the car, negotiate the gangs
Of pent-up children bursting free from school,
Jostling, swinging their satchels, unaware
That you are walking slowly up the hill.

The ancient car rolls on, no longer coughing . . .
Where shall I stop it? Where shall we two meet?
Let X denote the spot beyond the turning
Where you will sit beside me once again
And share a pause of truth, a wordless fragment
Snatched from time.
        The Thames is moving still:

The adolescent horde rampages on -
Unfit – as yet – to understand.
             I bless you,

Tall in your coat of green, and tired and gracious,
At one in death and life for good or ill,
Walking towards me, slowly, up the hill.

FOR A VALENTINE CARD

When I bought this
Two schoolgirls stood
Cards in hand.
One said she would

The other she wouldn't
Sign her name.
In a secret glance
They shared the game

Of guessing who liked them
Best of the boys:
Ah perilous
Uncharted joys!

Where gliding sharks
Haunt rock and reef
Rash mariners
May come to grief.

I made a wish
They too may know
Such love as we
Have witnessed grow

In children's eyes
In passing years,
In spite of pain,
In face of fears;

And learn to love
As you love me –
As long as rocks
Outface the sea.

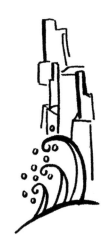

A SILVER DISH

for a silver wedding

I sent my dearest friend
A book of godly verse;
Primly against the trend –
For better or for worse.

When truth was truly tried
We shared a golden ring.
Desire was satisfied;
We triumphed, queen and king.

I give my trusted wife
A Roman silver dish:
Emblem of youth and life –
Pledge of my dearest wish:

For here the smith revealed
A naked lover dancing,
A maiden half-concealed:
Entranced – and still entrancing.

Thus holy and profane –
The loves of Christ and Pan –
Join hands and kiss again:
As we do, wife and man.

They, on the gleaming plate,
Share rhythm, limb and look.
Today we celebrate
The dish, the ring, the book.

*(The 'book of godly verse' is 'The Poems of George Herbert'.
The dish is a replica of part of the treasure found at Mildenhall
and now in the British Museum)*

A VALENTINE

while undergoing radiotherapy

The rays I cannot
Sense or see
Run through and through
Recumbent me . . .

I feel the buzz;
I hear the hum.
"Our Father,
May your kingdom come."

The gantry stirs
And moves. "Your will
Be done." . . . hum . . . buzz . . .
. . .While I lie still

And think how we
Played kiss and vow . . .
Who could foretell
The distant now?

The gantry stops.
The spell is cast.
This I declare:
The future, past

And present joys
We both possess
Outrun the rays
That burn and bless.

WEDDING GIFTS

THREE WISHES FOR A WEDDING

Firstly, we wish you both
The joy of one-in-two,
Beyond all telling true;
Flower of your happy youth.

Our second wish is peace,
With God for guarantee –
Peace of the One in Three,
As years and joys increase.

Lastly . . . below . . . above . . .
Within . . . without . . . around
May you be lost, and found
And crowned and clothed in love.

Peace, joy and love today
And onwards into life,
Be yours as man and wife . . .
We wish . . .
        We bless . . .
                We pray.

VERSES FOR THE WEDDING OF MARION AND TOM

"Sweet Thames, run softly till I end my song!" from
Prothalamion – a Spousal Verse by Edmund Spenser (1596)

Sweet Thames, run softly till I end my song.
We came from near and far
To witness Wandsworth's registrar
Declare these lovers wedded man and wife.
A job well done! No foot put wrong!
And now the bard must do the best he can.
Sweet Thames run softly till I end my song.

Sweet Thames, run softly while my song proceeds.
Crossing your muddy stream by various bridges
We saw no grassy banks or quivering reeds
Crowning the Surrey Shore.
Threatened by petrol fumes – not midges –
We fail to spot that 'store of vermeil roses
Or little daisy that at evening closes,'
But motored on from land to land,
Reaching the northern strand,
Where once adventurous longboats lay;
But now frustrated buses hum and roar.

Who cares? Let sage and serious Spenser fade away.
For this is Tom and Marion's wedding day.

Sweet Thames, run softly till I end my ditty.
We hand the mike to London's William Blake,
Who often did the Lambeth Walk,
And thought it simple commonsense to talk
With angels – not indeed, the social norm –
Glimpsing the great and good Unseen
Around the Echoing Green.
"For all" – says Blake – "must love the Human Form
In Heathen, Turk or Jew"
(And that means me and you).
Therefore let Peace and Mercy, Love and Pity –
To whom all pray in their distress –
Join happy hands and bless
Marion and Tom, and let their wise "I do"
Grow tall and straight and true
Till heart and mind and hand and eye unite,
Creating new delight.
For thus shall hurt be healed, despair transcended.
But look, the slow September sun goes down,
Gilding the groves and glades of Kentish Town.
Sweet Thames, run softly, for my song is ended.

A BLESSING FOR JANE AND JAMES

Weem Church, July 16th, 2005

Gracious Lord of light and life,
Make these lovers man and wife.

Rhyme a charm for Jane and James,
Blending souls and mingling names.
Think in faith – and see them wear
Garlands bright with honest prayer.

Gracious Lord of light and life,
Make these lovers man and wife.

Jane, when new and shy and small,
Smiled at flowers and loved them all.
James beside a Lakeland stream
Learnt to swim and fish and . . . dream.

Little darlings – how they grew!
What they put their parents through . . .
Infant wailings, bumps and grazes,
Tantrums maybe? Teenage phases . . .

Gracious Lord of light and life,
Make these lovers man and wife.

Jane delights in style and fashion
Warm with mercy and compassion.
James – who works at serious playing –
Makes a living while surveying.

Dashing James and Jane go skiing,
Daring, rarely disagreeing;
Now the compass marked 'for keeps'
Guides across uncharted deeps.

Gracious Lord of light and life,
Make these lovers man and wife.

God of grace – we dare detect you.
Let our loving still reflect you.
Make them wise through humdrum living,
Daily giving – and forgiving;

Richer, poorer, worse or better
Each the other's happy debtor.
Guard the vows of you-plus-me,
Tie the knot that sets them free.

Ring-for-ring shall serve as token:
Thus my charm is truly spoken..

Gracious Lord of light and life,
Make these lovers man and wife.

FOR THE WEDDING OF CARL AND NERIMAN

20 November 2004

Today you meet to make
The vows of man and wife,
Each for the other's sake
Entwining life with life:
A holy partnerhood,
For ever – and for good.

That friendly pledge, "I do",
Will often call again,
And gladly guide you through
The tangled paths of pain
And joy in life's dark wood,
For ever – and for good.

And God, so strangely living,
Whose love puts paid to fear,
Through giving and forgiving
Will make his purpose clear
When all is understood,
For ever – and for good.

THANKSGIVINGS

A THANKSGIVING FOR GOOD WORDS

Give thanks for words that rhyme and ring,
Sweet as a chiming bell;
For kind and courteous speech;
Give thanks for words that seem to sing,
For thoughtful words that teach
Us who we are, and show
Plain truths we need to know.
Give thanks for gentle words that say "I heard
You and I'm here.
No need to fear."
Give thanks for every good and honest word.

IN MEMORY OF I.D.,
WHO FELL IN THE BIAFRAN WAR

What was your heart's desire
As entrance tests went by;
And you would not retire
But get a form and try
Again and lick and stick the envelope,
Posting a youngster's badly battered hope?

What was your heart's desire
When nineteen years were passed?
Was youthful flesh on fire
To know a girl at last?
How shy you were . . . but strong to satisfy
A woman's need and soothe a baby's cry.

What was your heart's desire:
Drenched by the pitiless rain,
Fouled in the tropical mire
As the tanks crawled forward again?
Did you pray, my son, in faith or fear,
Before the bullet struck? And was He near?

My heart is sure of this:
A boy I was glad to know
Felt brief but valid bliss
Golden ages ago.
You dropped your bag and shouted "Here at last!"
And grinned and shook my hand and held it fast.

YOUNG SAMSON

"Samson . . . bowed with all his might . . . and the house fell."
(Judges 16:30)

Here are some things to make the baby laugh;
A plastic saucer balanced on his head
Suddenly tumbling down; a skein of wool
Dropped from a height and landing on his nose;
Coloured balls that he can grip in one
Small and clumsy hand . . . but these – forgive me –
Are now the stale pursuits of bygone days,
Several weeks ago. More daring deeds
Attract the hero now. Enormous volumes –
Cruden's Concordance and the works of Shakespeare –
Crash to the ground before him. Look! No hands –
Or just one hand, for safety's sake – he sways
On tiptoe spying out the kitchen table:
A snow-white plateau, vast, littered with booty:
Salt and pepper, mustard, sauce and pickle,
Knives, forks and spoons. Observe that dangerous eye,
Ready to drag the little world of lunch
In hideous ruin and confusion down.
Enough, young Samson, try your Teddy Bear
And leave the flex alone. Play with your toys –
Your toys, I tell you! Keep your temper, baby,
And I'll keep mine. O blithe and bonny child,
That ancient venturer brought destruction down
Upon his blinded head. May your bright eyes
Never be darkened by despair or guilt;
Your explorations lead you through the mist
To undiscovered country; leaping across
The stepping stones to upland valleys, may you
Find for yourself the rarest flowers of joy.

MOON! MOON!

Both of us saw the moon. It chased us home
Crouching behind the council houses; jumping
Over the dark dark trees. That solemn face
Calmly observed us walking up the drive;
It slid behind the racing clouds, and moved
Stealthily out again to watch us run
Up to the lighted house where mother lives.

I made my great discovery too: at teatime,
Before the curtains closed and television
Deadened the vast and breathing universe,
I saw you stand on tiptoe at the window –
Dear two-year old – searching your stock of words
And pointing, pointing at infinity.
"Moon! Moon!" you cried: I knelt beside you then
And saw the silver galleon sailing high
Over the garden shed for you alone.

That moon has looked on lovers, little son;
Has shone on battlefields. Unburied dead
Have stared at her. Enchanted generations
Of boys and girls have all come out to play
In coolest calmest moonlight. Even now
When monstrous lamp-posts make the street look sick
And television rants and roars, the moon
Can still enchant a child. My son, I wish
That I could still enjoy the world as you do.

THE WELSH CHAPEL

Uncertain now, I hardly dare
To go inside the chapel. Who
Knows the strangers lurking there?
They speak a foreign language too!
Your unrequired attentions vex;
Begone, ye touring rubbernecks.

Across the bay the mountains loom;
Dark, hung with heavy cloud. Among
Those crags ancestral kings found room
To guard the nation and the tongue,
There Owen, Prince of Wales, retreated;
By age and Saxon arms defeated.

O no! Communion! Let's get out!
Too late – I slide along a pew.
Striving to look Welsh and devout
Among the saints far-flung and few,
I contemplate the solemn faces
Of deacons taking proper places.

Lord, though I hardly heard the preacher
Speak of the cup, of blood and wine;
With even less success, true Teacher,
I make your secret language mine.
But still, I knew my sins were ended
When friendly natives weren't offended.

Outside the door, a speedboat-trailer
Frustrates a fuming traffic jam;
Soon shifted by a lady sailor
With many an English 'hell' and 'damn'.
Meanwhile, aware that God is nigh,
Backs to the wall the Welsh go by.

IN PRAISE OF MY AUNT, LENA LEE

(1902 – 1997)

My aunty is ninety. She lives by the sea,
And still she comes up with surprises for me.
With eatable treats she embellished my youth
And now she gives glimpses of Ultimate Truth.

I went down to Worthing on business . . . and thought
"She'll be just round the corner. Let's face it. I ought
To drop in." So I rang. "Someone's coming. Guess who!"
"But John, dear, my hairdresser's calling at two."

So the lady adjusted that helmet they use,
While Aunty and I exchanged family news
As I sat by the window and gazed at the sand
And the sky and the breakers that snarl at the land.

Her adventures with uncle – if turned into song –
Would prove – when performed – unacceptably long.
In Church and in State her track record is good
And she cared for the aged as long as she could.

(Now a word to my students – who may be perplexed
As Post Modernists keep Deconstructing the Text.
An encounter with Aunty will surely restore
Truth, Beauty and Goodness – as plain as before.)

Her frailty is bright with concern and with clarity.
Therefore I pen this short poem for charity.
Pay up – good people – and sponsor a rhyme
To join me in praising this Aunt of All Time.

(a Sponsored Poem for Christian Aid Week)

FAITH

"All you need is love" (The Beatles)
"Faith, hope and love remain" (St Paul)

Faith is one of several friends
Who's out of sync with current trends.

Faith defies Dishonest Doubt
And sees the lover in the lout;

Lets her offspring grow . . . and go . . .
But never says "I told you so."

Golden lads and girls are dust,
Subtle Faith transfigures lust.

Faith attempts the extra mile:
Faith befriends the paedophile.

Faith perverted leads to hell:
(Joseph Stalin knew it well.)

Faith bamboozled, in despair,
May require Intensive Care.

Humble faith – that holy fool –
Coaches duffers after school . . .

Love is all that Beatles need:
Faith will keep her up to speed.

Paul puts love at Number One:
Faith will make her run and run . . .
Outperforming stars and sun.

FOR A YORUBA NAMING CEREMONY

(written during the Nigerian Civil War)

Your Father named you 'Endless Joy';
At eight days old the rites were duly
Done. He wanted to beget a boy
But still he laughs and loves you truly.

The preacher called you 'Precious Lamb', and said
No-one could tell your worth in money.
He touched your lips with salt and red
Palm oil, sugar, bitter kola, honey,
Two drops of water, prayers to finish; then
The spell that binds you to the world of men
Was spun, and you were back in bed,
While we relaxed on wooden benches,
Our wants supplied by serving wenches:
Weak tea, and margarine on hunks of bread.

Be good in soul and fair of face,
Dear child of Oluduwa's race;
Grow lithe and wise and tall until
Young men will turn and gaze their fill;
With headtie at a gallant angle,
Your wrapper gaily tucked about your hips,
On each strong wrist a gilded bangle,
Your hair a plaited crown, your lips
Trembling and sensitive with love unwoken . . .
But that's enough –
Whether you marry in the ancient fashion
Or feel the sudden spring of passion
For some smart lad at College
With Parker pen and all; O not too rough
May your awakening be; still unbetrayed
Your trust – your loving unafraid;

Guiltless your tasting of the tree of knowledge
In full commitment of a heart unbroken.

Those silver birds that soar so high
Are Federal jets, my love; they tear the sky
In two above your head, and then
Away towards the East they fly
To roast and blast Ojukwu's men.
And little Ibo girls must die
Because of this, and mothers too.
So great a grief indeed that I
(Who know the rights and wrongs both sides maintain)
Cannot attempt to turn it into verse,
But only pray the young like you
May see poor tattered peace emerge again
From hiding; all our people from the curse
Of mutual fear and ignorance set free.
How happy I would be
To watch the girl for whom I sing
Dance with our Eastern maidens in a ring.

It looks as if a boil has come
Under your arm; poor soul, I'm sorry.
If only we could leave this slum
And pack our loads inside a lorry
And roll three hundred miles to grandpa's place . . .
Where families of ducks and pigs
Surround those houses dark and cool and strong.
Where cunning beauties smooth the face
With camwood, not with Astral Cream,
And fashion calls for beads, not wigs,
And boys and girls are happy all day long
Jumping and splashing in the stream,
And games on moonlit nights are overjoyed . . .
But if you finish school you're unemployed.

So here, alas, we have to stay -
Your father holds a job, which means a lot:
Beside a muddy street is where you play,
(Hair combed and neatly dressed,
For mother does her best)
Although the District Council quite forgot
To clear this heap of rotting fruit away.
So shall I now assign your Christian name?
(Esther, Elizabeth, Charity or Ruth?)
You have one, child: the very same
Your father gave is full of grace and truth.
Let endless joy be yours, as day by day
You walk the meadows of the happy mind
Among the lambs who never stray
Into the clutch of any evil power.
And in conclusion, this, I pray
May be, dear child, your wedding dower;

Not car or fridge or wealth of any kind,
Gold lace or spangled shoes to make you vain,
Instead, a bathroom and a hissing shower,
A small clean kitchen with a proper drain.
Mercies like these will set you free
When joy of your own sits laughing on your knee.

IN PRAISE OF HOPE

Hope is an unexpected letter:
"Hey, we love you – please get better."

Hope is a voice from long ago
Ringing up to say "hello".

Hope is a sunlit baby's room
Whose guest is dancing in the womb.

Hope is a young and puzzled brow;
A smile that says: "I get it now".

Hope turns up to sweep and scrub
When fools have vandalised the club.

Hope takes part in Sponsored Walks;
Hope puts up with boring talks.

Hope is a well that's truly sunk,
Healthy water gladly drunk.

Faith and Love are Jack and Jill.
Hope will help them up the hill.

Hope is . . . hope is . . . what you will.

AN INCANTATION AGAINST DEHYDRATION, AND IN PRAISE OF THE UNICEF 'ORAL REHYDRATION THERAPY' SPOON.

*(first performed at the 'Avery Hill for Ethiopia' concerts,
January 28 and 29 1988)*

SUGAR, SALT AND WATER MIX:
GIVE THE FEEBLE CHILD A FIX.

Get the combination right:
Dull young eyes, be brave and bright!

Double-ended plastic spoon,
Work a wonder – do it soon!

First the crystals – then the grains:
Ease the twisted body's pains.

Make the measure smooth and level:
Thus we scotch the burning devil!

How much water? Just a litre!
Add the sugar – make it sweeter:

Add the salt to make it stronger.
Drink, my darling dear: live longer!

Water, sugar, salt prevail:
Listless baby – learn to wail!

SUGAR, SALT AND WATER MIX:
GIVE THE FEEBLE CHILD A FIX.

Angry aircraft, split the sky!
Drop us sugar bombs – we cry.

Tanks and armoured legions – halt!
Squad – salute a sack of salt!

Three in one are truly blended,
Death's dictatorship is ended.

SUGAR, SALT AND WATER MIX:
GIVE THE FEEBLE CHILD A FIX.

Bless the mixture: stir it well.
Restless baby, learn to yell!

SUGAR, SALT AND WATER MIX:
GIVE THE FEEBLE CHILD A FIX.

Last of all – get rid of greed:
Then the charm is good indeed.

SUGAR, SALT AND WATER MIX:
GIVE THE FEEBLE CHILD A FIX.

IN PRAISE OF SAPPHO

Little is known of Sappho.
This poem uses the metre to which she gave her name.

Sappho, dear mistress of long lost poetry,
Lady of Lesbos, so little remembered,
How many verses, flawlessly crafted
Perished for ever?

Though we can find them only in fragments
Faded and brittle, yet we perceive that
Glimpses of beauty can bring you before us:
Sappho entirely.

A WORD OF THANKS TO ALEXANDER RUBY

Alexander Ruby was born in Thurso. He was a lifelong Salvationist, and a virtuoso on the cornet. After war service in the Marines, he gave his time freely to aspiring young musicians in the 'learners class'.

The 'word of thanks' was written for his funeral in July 1990.

"Slow melodies" – you said – "are best.
A simple solo folk enjoy."
You were a man and I a boy.
Thirteen, perhaps? I was impressed.

How else – indeed – would I recall
Your words from forty years ago?
So painfully we learned to blow:
So patiently you taught us all.

Of every subtle semi-quaver
You were – of course – an honoured master.
Your fingers flickered faster, faster . . .
I never knew your goodness waver.

"Fight the good fight with all thy might . . . "
Our tunes came very slow at first:
Sharps, flats and brackets did their worst:
We fought them every Thursday night.

A sergeant, you withdrew from Greece.
The angry Stukas shrieked and dived.
A piper answered: you survived . . .
Oh, lived . . . I give you thanks and peace . . .

To teach us crotchets, minims, scales,
Hymn tunes, marches, then SELECTIONS!
Survived our childish close inspections . . .
Love . . . you suggested . . . never fails.

Now, at long last, a few bars rest?
So pack the cornet in its case.
And greet your Master, face to face.
Slow melodies – indeed – are best.

A SCHOLAR REMEMBERED

Dr Marinell Ash was one of those forthright, immensely civilised American scholars who made her British counterparts seem timid and provincial by comparison . . . She developed a passion for Scottish history . . . She saw her death . . . as an annoying obstacle to getting on with the fun of rooting around . . . history and sharing it . . . with the next generation.

Robin Bell in 'The Scotsman'

A land you left; a land you found.
From California first you came
To camp on Caledonian ground,
Tracking the past for fun and fame.
Our Scotland, then, you loved the best . . .
Or was it still the wild wild West?

You met me at the B.B.C.
And bade me cross a magic border
Into school at Merrilee,
Slung with a heavy tape recorder,
To chase the skipping game, the rhyme
That plays at hide-and-seek with time.

How skilled you were to think and feel!
The broch, the weathered symbol-stone.
The shabby wynd, the ruined peel:
All these you loved and made your own.
An airless close, a tumbled cairn
Revealed the man, the wife, the bairn.

So shall this Ancient Kingdom say
She found a friend who loved her well:
The haunted stones of Skara Brae
Shall stand in praise of Marinell
Who casts her fragile pain behind –
A land to leave: a land to find.

IN MEMORY OF WALTER ALLEESON

Treasurer of The Salvation Army, Ealing Citadel

You kept the books – and kept them straight,
Which I could never hope to do.
Nothing missing – never late:
A weekly wonder, baffling, true.
You kept the books, and kept them straight.

Receipts and vouchers all in place,
Paraded, drilled, inspected, filed:
The Cash Books in a state of grace,
All disagreements reconciled –
Receipts and vouchers all in place.

The Heavenly Host will think it funny
(Funny-good, not funny-odd)
To think you worked for joy not money,
For love of man, in praise of God.
The Heavenly Host will think it funny.

Well done, thou good and faithful friend!
– 'Faithful servant', don't you mean? –
It's 'friend' not 'servant' in the end:
See John fifteen, and verse fifteen.
Well done, thou good and faithful friend!

So says our Lord: I say the same.
Let those who shared your pain and fun
Whisper a dearer, sweeter name.
For me the word is 'Friend, well done!'
So says our Lord. I say the same.

"Well done, thou good and faithful servant" – *Matthew 25:21*
"Henceforth I call you not servants, but I have called you friends"
    – *John 15:15*

146

IN MEMORY OF SIOBHAN MCNULTY

(written for the Avery Hill College Review, June 13 1990)

Across the stillness be my friend:
Your face, your voice I scarcely knew.
They organised a cool revue.
Like all good shows, it had to end.

The plan: to help St Bob's relief.
Some of the acts were really funny;
You raised an awful lot of money . . .
But then, the strange unscheduled grief . . .

When I enquired, she wasn't there . . .
Who can interpret how or why
The young and energetic die?
A single truth I dare declare:

The good that women do lives after:
For now, in Somewhere Far Away
The boys and girls come out to play
And you are praised in children's laughter,

Honoured in squabbles, blessed in fun . . .
Perhaps you gave them . . . half a breath?
They dance without a thought of death.
The sun goes down: the rivers run.

Siobhan was a student at Avery Hill. She organised two major
fund-raising events – the 'Avery Hill for Ethiopia' concerts
on January 28 and 29 1988. 'St Bob' is Sir Bob Geldof.

THREE POEMS AT THE BERLIN WALL
EASTER 1990

*"Living within the truth . . . is a moral act . . . an attempt to
gain control over one's own sense of responsibility."*

Vaclav Havel: 'The power of the powerless'

PRESENT   A Blessing for a Living Child

You spied a place to play:
A strip of smooth and open sand:
You were the one that didn't get away,
A young policeman grabbed your small
Protesting hand . . .
And how we all
Chuckled to see the sheepish infant-carrier
Hand you back to mum across the barrier.

This was the killing zone:
Here you explored alone,

Rushing in where fools would fear to tread:
And thus
Dear child –
You blessed the cheated dead.

PAST An Incantation for the Dead

Sullen souls, be still at last;
Here I pour a gourd of verse,
Soothe the poor demented past;
Slay the spell, unsay the curse.

Now is Hitler's rasping rant
Rightly rumbled, truly done:
Here a cross marked 'Unbekannt'
Keeps an eye on Easter fun.
Kaiser Wilhelm, lead the way!
Yours the plume, the sweat, the cheers.
Let the merry marches play;
Greet the jolly, ghostly faces:
Now farewell – resume your places:
Fill the land of long ago . . .
(Still the bands perspire and blow
Tootling, fading one by one)

Take my words instead of tears.

FUTURE Writing on the Wall

(an inscription for the unborn)

When you come out to play
I shall be far away,
Dear children, still to be . . .
What can I say?
Remember Adolf? Make a note of me?
Don't overdo
The history thing – but still, it's wise and kind
To keep the poor old past in mind.
I wish I'd got the chance to spray
My words of wisdom on that grotty wall
Before its final fall!
Here's the graffito, pals, from us to you
From age to youth.

WANNA BE FREE?
YA GOTTA LIVE IN TRUTH

That's all . . .
That's all . . .

IN MEMORY OF SIR JOHN BETJEMAN
– POET LAUREATE

In amazement I saw Sir John Betjeman coming
Encased in full armour of piston and wheel.
He stopped at the platform, triumphantly humming:
His name was emblazoned in letters of steel.

Unspeakable power from an overhead cable
Had brought him to Glasgow, bisecting the day:
A knight all-electric . . . yet oddly unable
To reason, to rhyme, to perceive, or to pray.

Did you see on T.V.? When his engine was christened
Our chivalrous poet in person was there.
While speeches were made, he sat silent and listened:
They wheeled him away in a practical chair.

Now the bard has been buried: his namebearer thunders
And whines in high triumph by Beattock and Shap.
The man has bequeathed us a box of bright wonders:
One day the poor train will be shunted to scrap.

So if any should dare to belittle his verses,
Or slander his fame before ages to come,
I shall crush the base critic with metrical curses . . .
His motto was mercy; let malice be dumb.

I salute you, Sir John, now promoted to glory:
Your prayers were perceptions, your reasonings rhyme.
The bruised and the broken may learn from your story
To triumph *(pro tem)* over ominous time.

JOY IN JINGLING

To call on Jeremy James
I chose the shortest day
(But over the soggy Essex fields
The winter sunshine lay).

Jeremy too lay flat,
At less than five months old -
But his eyes were bright and his legs were strong
And his fingers – brave and bold.

So I wound his humming top:
Like a world it span and swayed,
As Jeremy struggled and struggled to see:
Defeated – undismayed.

Then, as we said goodbye,
I jangled my bunch of keys
Before his nose – O startled face!
What sights – what sounds were these?

Such music and such art
Were never known before!
He laughed and unfurled his exquisite hands
As I stood beside the door.

So I ask for Jeremy James
Increasing joy in jingling
Till – why not Mozart, MAGIC FLUTE? –
Sets feet and fingers tingling.

May sudden gleams of light
Surprise his growing youth
Till REMBRANDT – there's the man for me! –
Reveals a deeper truth!

And so shall Jeremy James
To wisest manhood grow:
And make another baby laugh
When I lie still and low.

IN MEMORY OF A QUAKER FRIEND

The books you loved
And left behind
Recall your life,
Reveal your mind.

Prizes wear
The Old School Crest:
English poets –
They were best.

You chose them young –
Perceptive boy! –
They loved you long,
Bestowing joy,

Words beyond words,
Elusive truth.
And shared the trek
To age from youth

As down the years
You added slim
Volumes of verse
(Whose sales were grim)

And travelled far,
Daring to reach
Remotest realms
Beyond all speech,

In Meeting Time,
When words were stilled,
God was adored,
And you fulfilled.

Now these dumb poets,
Shelf on shelf,
Whisper to me
"See for yourself!

This Friend perceived
Innermost light!
Go on . . . We dare you!
Write, man, write."

Therefore I spill
The subtle wine
Of words before
This wooden shrine.

THE GREAT LEAP FORWARD

You took a piece of plastic from the dresser
And tried to wipe your brother's tears away.
The well-bumped head was four years old: the ill-
Controlled and clumsy hands were less than two.
You almost wiped his eyes, and having done so,
Dropped the crumpled plastic on the floor,
Forgotten.

      This, my son of several words,

I shan't forget. This was your first observed
Unselfish act. I watch you in the garden,
Feeling the grass between your toes. Already
You give unguarded love. At nineteen months
The wobbly child aspires to play the man.

SPONSORED WALKER

Twelve year old Jane is my pop personality,
Free from all malice, all grief and all guile.
When she says "Hi!" I forget man's mortality.
Jane I have sponsored at tuppence a mile.

Jane is as bright as a highlander's hackle;
First on the soccer field, eager to go.
Fair hair a-flying she speeds to the tackle:
Lumbering louts she despoils and lays low.

Jane is my friend, though a little disparity
Plainly distinguishes Wisdom from Youth.
Jane plans to walk in support of some charity.
Would I go with her . . . ? I tell you the truth.

JANE HAS INVITED ME. Don't say I dreamt it!
What though the path may be hilly and hard,
Show me the mountain – with Jane I'll attempt it.
You, Sir, will sponsor me. FILL IN MY CARD!

RECALLED IN JOY . . .

An empty road: intimidating palm trees;
Heat and humidity: the tarmac shimmering;
Nothing on wheels in sight – my journey broken
And fifteen miles to go . . .
Exasperation soaked in perspiration . . .

But then, a still, small voice, behind, below me:
"Father, sit down!" A shy and solemn child
Offers a home-made stool, unasked, unprompted,
In form and face and word entirely gentle . . .
I wield my best linguistic skills, but either
Respect for elders or my dubious accent
Puts paid to dialogue: the rest is silence.

Dear friends,
(Dear Lord and Friend – I count you in)
For some the gifts come thick and fast at Christmas:
There's gold, and frankincense, and aftershave
And myrrh, and monthly magazine subscriptions . . .
But look! I've brought a rarity to show:
One simple act of utmost innocence
Recalled in joy from thirty years ago.

FOR FATHER ANGELO

*who planted a tree in Ethiopia in memory of every soul
who perished in the famine*

A living tree for every death:
For every cry a quivering leaf:
A searching root for every grief:
A bud for every searing breath:
A green and wordless requiem
Sung in the wind – for all of them . . . ?

They gave the viewing world a shock
On TV news, in '88:
"Too late" – says dirty dust – "too late:
The tender seedlings merely mock . . .
Come off it! Father Angelo!
You saw them die – so you should know."

I wandered down the lane in Kent
As fragile hawthorn blossoms fell:
The grasses whispered: all is well . . .
Our elm and ash were also meant
To bless the unrecorded dead,
Now, and when all is done and said.

Meanwhile, fresh boys and girls come out
To grace the Ethiopian green:
So good and glad a rural scene
Casts light on life, and doubt on doubt.
I place my bet on Angelo:
He saw it through, and he should know.

VIDEO CONFERENCE

I saw you smile on video
And weave a small uncertain hand,
Sending a tentative hello
Prepackaged over sea and land.
I saw you smile on video.

The birthday party took its course.
The paper-hatted pals ran free;
As mums and dads grew hot and hoarse
You stopped, and spoke to missing me.
The birthday party took its course.

How strange a puzzle! Where was I?
The gleaming lens, as go-between,
Aided papa to ratify
Our league of love, alive, unseen.
How strange a puzzle! Where was I?

We hold our aging breath: it's you!
No doubt about it. Spools of tape
Transmit the beautiful, the true,
The smiling soul, the growing shape:
We hold our ageing breaths: it's you!

Long may she reign, in Year the Third.
Grandpa is running short of time:
Offscreen indeed, but not unheard,
He sends a blessing wrapped in rhyme.
Long may she reign, in Year the Third!

CHRISTMAS INTERPRETED

THE MAD WOMAN'S BLESSING
ON THE CHRIST CHILD

My curses on King Cruelty.
His eyes are dull and dead.
His guards are armed with anger;
He rules the land of dread.

Love to the Lord of Nowhere
Whom nothing can destroy.
He and his friends from Everywhere
Shall share the land of joy.

I wish for newest children
Who face the faceless years,
No hatred in their laughter;
No terror in their tears.

I pray for all good people
With nothing left to give.
O go and give your nothing,
And learn to love and live.

For once the King of Everywhere
Has bound the Lord of Dread,
Your nothing shall be everything;
Your stone shall turn to bread.

THE KING OF HEART'S DESIRE

John the Baptist said: "After me will come
One who is mightier than I . . ." (Mark 1:7)

O beware of the King of Heart's Desire:
He will drench your dreams in sensational fire:

He will hose you down to the guilty skin,
And soak your souls to eliminate sin.

So cancel the Presidential Suite:
He comes to wash the beggarman's feet;

And tear those two-faced billboards down:
He plans to visit your shanty town.

Be sure of this: the great I AM
Is not impressed by plausible sham.

The Prince of Peace will bring to heel
All who attempt to wheel or deal:

But for those whose hearts are open and kind
His word is "Watch. You may happily find

In the hesitant smile of the nameless Other
A long-lost sister: a brand-new brother."

I clear the way. The king comes after:
His crown is adorned with innocent laughter.

So stop! Abandon cant! Repent!
Prepare for the Lord of Heart's Content.

A CAROL INTERRUPTED

"Helicopter gunships over Bethlehem"
(newspaper headline – November AD 2000)

"Angels from the realms of glory
Wing your flight o'er all the earth . . ."
War repeats its dreary story
Desecrates Messiah's birth.

"Shepherds in the field abiding . . ."
Watch the helicopter's flight.
Better keep your hopes in hiding,
Dodge the bleak and blinding light.

"Saints before the altar bending
Watching long in hope . . ." *and dread;*
Is a broken world worth mending?
Are your dreams for ever dead?

"Sages, leave your contemplations",
Hate and fear deface the ground;
While the Disunited Nations
Push the paperwork around . . .

"Sinners moved by true repentance
Doomed by guilt . . ." *to stress and strife:*
Hear the infant Word give sentence;
"I shall die to bring you Life."

Lord, a single prayer rings true:
"Forgive, we know not what we do."

(James Montgomery's Christmas hymn 'Angels from the realms of
glory' was first published in the Sheffield Iris on Dec. 24th 1816)

THE SOUND OF MUSIC

Remember 'The Sound of Music'?
That film with 'do-re-mi'?
Vivacious Julie Andrews
Delightful to hear and see?

Von Trapps – that Holy Family –
Were driven to run away
Or sing for Adolf Hitler,
And sell their souls for pay.

Remember the scene that caught them
Cold in the headlight's glare?
Gestapo agents shouting
"Freeze! Just hold it there!"

They froze indeed – and mighty dread
Did seize their troubled mind.
Bad tidings of great hate were brought
To them and all mankind.

So was it like that by Bethlehem?
"Hold it, shepherds, freeze!"
Someone or something luminous
Leaving them weak at the knees?

Drilled by a laser beam of light?
Caught on the cruel hop?
Itching, twitching, squinting,
Wanting the joke to stop?

Blinking in bewilderment,
Wondering "What the hell?"
"Don't panic, lads!" – that Something said,
"Glad tidings I do tell."

It isn't 'beggar your neighbour',
Or 'Glory be to Greed!'
It's 'Unto-us-a-child-is-born' –
Now there's the news you need.

It's not 'Hurrah for Herod!'
Or 'Romans rule, OK!'
It's just a vagabond infant,
Economically wrapped in hay.

A social call in Bethlehem
Should deal with any doubt:
Go, shepherds, go – with attitude –
And quickly check it out!

Cue in the Sound of Music.
Cross fade the Heavenly Chorus!
Fast forward through the centuries . . .
Beware what lies before us.

Beware of Ethnic Cleansing,
With droves of refugees:
Beware of Global Warming
– You either fry or freeze.

Beware of Nuclear Fallout,
In case it lands on you . . .
Father, forgive our follies:
We know not what we do.

Rewind the tape to Bethlehem:
Where else can sinners go?
Freeze-frame the Christ in close-up:
Be still, dear friends and know . . .

The light is warm and gentle.
Remove your shades – if any –
This child is like no other.
This child is one of many.

The only radiation here
Is God's intensive grace:
It pierces mind and marrow
Through time and thought and space.

So fade the angry hubbub
Of hateful hell – and cue
The sound of silent music.
I hear it, friends . . . can you?

GROWING

Jesus said, "Consider the lilies of the field . . ."
(Matthew 6:28)

First a seedling
Falls asleep,
Then a root
Burrows deep.
Now a shoot
Greeny-white
Curls and twirls
Towards the light.

Tendrils creep
Down below;
Stem and branches
Breathe and grow.
Leaves alive
Sway and thrive:
Water, air
And earth prepare . . .

Now the flower
Pale and blue
Enjoys her hour:
And so can you . . .

THE CHILD IN NEED

A prayer – and a response

God of unimagined space
Far beyond our deepest dreaming:
Now we see Your glory gleaming
In a homeless baby's face:
Can so strange a plan succeed?
– *Welcome, Jesus, child in need.*

Word eternal, known at last:
Answer plainly when we doubt you;
Should we try to live without you -
Still surprise us: heal our past...
"Lord, we love..." is all our creed.
– *Welcome, Jesus, child in need.*

Holy Spirit, see us here
(Thoughts adrift, and motives mixed)
Let our frail desires be fixed
On the love that conquers fear:
Set us free from guilt and greed.
– *Welcome, Jesus, child in need.*

God the Father, Spirit, Son,
May your broken world be mended,
Pain relieved, and foes befriended
By a Christmas well begun.
Make us glad in word and deed.
– *Welcome, Jesus, child in need.*

STANDARD REPORT ON ANY DISASTER

We've got the death rate down to ten percent.
This, you may feel, is ten percent too many.
But thank you, friends, for every pound and penny.
Be sure your gifts are well and wisely spent.

Perhaps you wonder where the money went?
We try to reach the place of greatest need
With grain and powdered milk. So kindly read
The interim report I now present.

Those media comments we may well resent.
'Poor paperwork and misdirected pity'
Appears a sad reward for your committee,
Which welcomes queries if sincerely meant.

It's Christmas, friend . . . a long way off from Lent.
But why not spare a prayer, or stop and think,
Forego a little food, a drop of drink,
And make today a truly great event?

I call you all to holy discontent.
Let's get the death rate down from ten . . . to five . . . ?
May sleepy children rest in peace, alive,
And mother's lullaby replace lament.

CHRISTMAS DAY IS GOOD FOR BUSINESS!

(A true story – it happened in Lagos, Nigeria)

Twisted, distorted beggar man!
He crawls with clogs on hands and knees.
Observe his features if you can.
Improve his prospects as you please.
Here is a thing a saint would hiss . . .
Young Son of God, you came for this.

The office workers hurried out;
The office workers hurried in.
Could they avoid that crouching tout?
Their pennies hit – or missed – his tin.
Young Jesus, blessed by Mary's kiss –
Could you be born for such as this?

The Christians planned a Christmas feast,
And did the true disciple's duty,
Calling the lone, the lame, the least
To come and share donated booty.
A fleeting taste of endless bliss . . .
Who dares, dear Lord, to sneer at this?

The crooked beggar answered "No!
Today of days I make the most."
– He smiled a gentle smile – "And so
I simply daren't desert my post.
The trade is far too good to miss,"
Lord, did you die to deal with this?

THE WISE MEN INTERVIEWED

"Being warned in a dream not to return to Herod . . .
the wise men . . . departed to their own country by another way."
(Matthew 2:7,12)

How was your journey – we hope not too stressful?
Was it so wise to go chasing a star?
Thank you: our search was entirely successful.
Seeking a saviour we travelled afar.

Did you ask Herod the King to advise you?
He can deploy a whole army of spies . . .
Yes, we met Herod, but – does it surprise you? –
Chose to ignore his deplorable lies.

Where was this outhouse? A strange destination!
Did you miscalculate? Were you misled?
Sir, we homed in on a silent sensation:
There lay the treasure – asleep in a shed.

You had the treasure, or so goes the story,
Frankincense – was it – and myrrh and fine gold?
Nothing could equal the young Lord of glory,
Wrapped in warm loving to keep out the cold.

Is he a puppet-prince set up to fool us?
Someone's behind it: what funds have they got?
God is the schemer: his mercy will rule us
Truth is the programme, and peace is the plot.

Peace may be promised, but what is intended?
Death to King Herod? A challenge to Rome?
Slowly and surely the world will be mended:
Such was the promise that guided us home.

Be more specific, and tell us precisely
What your small Saviour proposes to do.
'Joy to all nations' will do very nicely.
Time will tell all, friend, to doubters like you.

THE OLD CARDBOARD CRIB

The cut-out shed is badly bent.
Poor tab-less Joseph totters down:
The Third Wise Man has lost his crown;
Time has been spent

And sticky tape consumed. The Lord
Wedged in his crib looks ill at ease.
A shepherd sags on well-worn knees.
Could we afford

To welcome Yule with something new?
Plastic, perhaps? That one-eared cow . . .
Can she be worth the effort now?
The time, the glue?

Beware! A long decade of dreams
Has blessed the shapes we half-condemn.
Behind our fragile Bethlehem
A candle gleams.

Therefore attend, observe, perceive.
We too are tatty, frail, absurd.
Our Christ is no mere makebelieve:
This cardboard Word.

AT LAST! THE VIRGIN MARY AGREES TO HOLD A PRESS CONFERENCE FOR THE MODERN MEDIA

"Mary treasured up all these things and pondered them in her heart" (Luke 2:19)

Peace to you all! How good to meet you,
Friends beyond our strangest dreaming.
What a shameful way to greet you!
Shock and screaming!

Please forgive our lack of manners!
Talking box and shining light
Made us think of Roman banners –
Gave us a fright.

I'll gladly answer, friends – but must
I go through labour pains again?
With us such things are not discussed
Before mere men.

"Was it a virgin birth?"
                    O dear . . .
Your shining eye and magic speakers
Dragged through time – are these the gear
Of scandal-seekers?

I shared my truth with Luke – that Greek
Who wrote the gospel – also Acts.
He's a recording man – so seek
And find the facts.

I felt the angel come and go.
(Angels to us are plain as flowers)
Dear Luke wrote all you need to know
Of those strange hours.

"So would you say you felt . . . impressed?"
We speak of wonder, joy and fear.
I simply said I'd do my best.
And God drew near . . .

"Joseph?"
My man was fair to me.
He prayed a lot: at times he spoke,
And many an ox in Galilee
Wears his kind yoke.

"Three kings? Please comment!"
                            Why go on
Yapping like dogs to kill my story?
One lily shows up Solomon
In all his glory!

Look at the birds who never spin
Or plough or sow or reap or store!
They bless my work, and help me win
My bread. I bore

The Living Word . . .
                            "Or so they say!"
Suppose I answer: "Yes, it's true!"
Will we be moved to pray – or pay?
How sad, if you

Who fly from earth to moon to earth,
Who speak across the empty skies
Should miss the point of this good birth,
Of my sharp cries . . .

(No, no, we won't discuss the labour)
I wish you'd learn from my dear Son . . .
Love God, and try to like your neighbour,
For every one

Of his wise tales contains the splendid
Truth the angel shared with me
Of man's primeval sorrow ended:
A world set free . . .

To find the facts in then and there,
You fly to ask me When? and How?
Go back and search your everywhere,
Your here and now.

A listening box may still discover
My child in unexpected places
So seek him out – your lord and lover –
In human faces.

"The crucifixion? No regret?"
Some truths are far too hard to tell.
Go now – the sun begins to set . . .
Go wise. Go well.

A FEW THOUGHTS FROM JOSEPH

At my time of life . . .
Just imagine the talk about me and my wife:
"So why did old Joseph get married?" they said.
"He had plenty to do in his carpenters shed . . ."
I'd hammer a plank and keep perfectly calm
And murmur a prayer or a favourite psalm . . .
But some of their comments can cut like a knife
At my time of life.

At my time of life –
So I carved a small crib with my chisel and knife . . .
Dear Mary – her thoughts are as deep as a well,
As cool as clear water and sweet as a bell . . .
And her soul is as quick and as bright as a bird . . .
Who can see what she sees? Who knows what she's heard?
So why should I worry if rumours are rife
At my time of life?

At my time of life
Corruption is public . . . and rotten . . . and rife . . .
If only the Romans would get off our backs:
They treat us like termites and tag us for tax . . .
And what if my Mary should go into labour?
Could anyone here play the part of good neighbour?
I should have got used to confusion and strife
At my time of life.

At my time of life . . .
We'll soon be delivered from sorrow and strife:
The good Lord has a purpose – as yet unrevealed:
I know – but my leathery lips are well sealed;
Now listen: the Kings of this World could all go –
There are secrets too sacred for Caesar to know;
I can laugh at his kettledrum, trumpet and fife
At my time of life.

At my time of life . . .
Well, we danced at our wedding – to tabor and fife.
And I've dreamt my own dream – it was ever so sweet.
I recall . . . I reflect . . . I refuse to repeat:
You ask me no questions: I tell you no lies,
But the child of my Mary could spring a surprise;
So I'm proud to be Joseph – the Man with a Wife –
At my time of life.

THE GENUINE CASE

A word of explanation from the innkeeper –
"There was no room for them in the inn" (Luke 2:7)

The genuine case!
It's hard to be sure from the look on a face.
All kinds come and knock on the door of my inn.
We get tricksters and scroungers as crooked as sin:
But when we say "no", we refuse with civility.
If "yes", then we never admit liability.
Strangers from Nazareth – what could I do?
(Of course, friends, we'd never inflict them on you!)
But duty demands that we find a small space
For the genuine case.

That genuine case!
The lies they can tell are a perfect disgrace!
Dear guests, take no notice – proceed with your dinner.
My inn has a welcome for saint and for sinner.
The census! Poor Bethlehem's packed to the door;
Out there in the courtyard you can't see the floor.
He's a northerner – accent incredibly thick!
(Though that in itself doesn't prove it's a trick)
And strong arms of charity always embrace
The genuine case.

O the genuine case!
They can pocket your money and sink without trace . . .
But the woman's expecting – that's obvious enough –
And the husband's a carpenter – hands very rough.
I thought we were faced with a forcible entry.
"Not in here, lad!" says I. "It's reserved for the gentry."
That soon stopped him blustering – not that I blame him.
A father-to-be, first time round! Who could shame him?
"Calm down, now" – says I – "We can always find space.
For the genuine case."

The genuine case!
I used to hunt swindlers for fun of the chase.
But now – in a crisis – we help if we're able.
I managed to find them a place in the stable:
A commonplace couple called . . . Joseph and Mary . . .
Some staff, I suspect, would be rather more wary.
But we can take care of disruptive behaviour.
It's part of my job to be godfather, saviour
Or nursemaid – forgetting religion and race –
To the genuine case.

The genuine case . . .
If he's telling the truth he's a long way from base.
I told her the baby could sleep in the manger.
. . . They're used to it, madam, there isn't much danger . . .
And all that it took was one look at his wife.
Of course, she could die on us – that's part of life;
But frankly, the house has got little to fear,
For I made our position abundantly clear:
No comeback on us – it's a gift of pure grace
To the genuine case.

A WORD FROM THE
CAMEL DRIVER'S MATE . . .

*"The visitors from the east . . . went into the house and when they saw
the child with his mother Mary, they knelt down and worshipped him.
They brought out their gifts of gold, frankincense and myrrh, and
presented them to him . . ."* (Matthew 2:7,11)

I'm just the camel driver's mate
That keeps the desert fleet afloat.
It's not my fault the party's late.
(Recording angel – kindly note!)
I'm just the camel driver's mate.

My masters made a stupid error:
They stopped in town – I thought it odd –
And asked your Herod – Lord of Terror –
To help locate the Son of God.
My masters made a stupid error.

But now – at last – they're safe inside.
Our Three Wise Men – three KINGS to you! –
Have swallowed camel-loads of pride...
Could such a crazy dream be true?
But now, at last, they're safe inside.

Hail to the Lord of life and light!
Our gifts have gone (it makes me wild:
I had to guard them day and night!)
To homeless Jesus – outhouse child.
Hail to the Lord of life and light!

But frankly, friends, I just don't care.
And you aren't here to kneel and pray.
You only came to stand and stare
At funny men from far away;
So frankly, friends, I just don't care.

In fact, I hope this IS the place!
X marks the spot where God – or Jove –
Who spins that star in outer space –
Conceals his priceless Treasure Trove.
In fact, I hope this IS the place . . .

A BLESSING FOR CHRISTMAS MORNING

The slow warm wave of sleep began to move
Silently back.
I felt the bulging bumpy sack
Standing beside

The bed: my childish puzzled hand inspected
Lumps, corners, shapes.
Ribbons and knotted strings and tapes –
Odd, unexpected –

Caressed me through the swollen pillow-case.
Suddenly, truth –
Pure – as perceived by saint or youth –
Made my heart race.

I saw the light, as bright as noonday sun!
HE had been there!
Bringing requested gifts most rare
To me, the one

And only Christmas child: Fumbling again,
Still half in doubt,
My hesitating hands made out
The clockwork train:

Key, pistons, wheels – O long-deferred desire!
Friend, may your joy
Be, like the thanks of one small boy,
Whole, good, entire.

A WORD FROM THE SCEPTICAL SHEPHERD . . .

"The shepherds said to one another: Let's go to Bethlehem."
(Luke 2:15)

I never went to Bethlehem.
I stayed behind to watch the sheep.
Glad tidings? Just the job for them;
But I – for one – was short of sleep.
I never went to Bethlehem.

The rest ran off to see the sight.
I stood alone to guard my post.
It's true – there was a kind of light
That could have been the Holy Ghost.
The rest ran off to see the sight.

They all returned, alive with joy,
Claiming an unexpected king.
A far from likely peasant boy . . .
I didn't have the heart to sing.
They all returned, alive with joy.

They tell me not to drift and doubt.
This poor-but-honest Prince of Peace
Has plans too big to leave me out.
Goodwill to all shall never cease.
They tell me not to drift and doubt.

Young god, so odd, here's half a prayer
From me: Let rarest grace anoint
The eyes of those who stand and stare
And always seem to miss the point.
Young god, so odd, here's half a prayer.

KING HEROD JOINS THE CAMPAIGN AGAINST LANDMINES

"Herod . . . gave orders to kill all the boys in Bethlehem . . . who were two years old and under . . ." (Matthew 2:16)

I always acted for the best:
Succeeding to the Jewish throne
I set myself a simple test:
The People's Welfare – not my own.
I always acted for the best.

The tale you hear is largely true:
Three odd astrologers inquire
About a 'King' (I wouldn't do.
To hell with fools who play with fire!)
The tale you hear is largely true.

We planned a clean and sudden strike
To target only infant males:
Do call it murder if you like:
But what if Public Order fails?
We planned a clean and sudden strike.

When whispered rumours get to Rome
Caesar's response is rather brisk:
He burns you out of house and home,
And older girls are then at risk –
When whispered rumours get to Rome.

So let me serve as bogey still
In gospel, sermon, song and play.
Your cunning little mines can kill
More kids than Herod any day.
So let me serve as bogey still.

But spare a thought – or prayer – for me:
Suppose he really was "The One
Whom prophets said would set us free . . ."
Reflect: just what would you have done?
And spare a thought – or prayer – for me.

THE FACE AT THE WINDOW

Is there a single soul alive
In all this god-forsaken street?
A scratch brass band with aching feet
Will now proclaim to Cedar Drive

Glad tidings of a Saviour's birth.
One startled cat appears to care.
Suburban souls sit warm and stare
At Television News . . . of earth

Battered and bombed and hijacked till
Commercials blandly ease the pain.
"Pay us to go away again"
Thinks Second Horn – he's feeling ill . . .

But now appears a single light
High in the grim and gloomy house.
Quick as a bird, shy as a mouse,
A child beholds the wondrous sight;

With small uncomprehending face
He sees the gleaming ring below.
Awaiting sound, he won't let go
That golden bear. Inspired, the bass

Booms boldly into 'First Noel'.
The drummer mutters "Umpteenth Time!"
While Cornet mounts to heights sublime
And scales the cruel summit well.

Look up, cold-hearted, iceberg-eared!
The icon in the window frame
Should set your ashen hearts aflame
As when the warning star appeared.

The child that holds the teddy bear
Calls to your mind the Son and Mother:
Look up, look down; observe each other,
In mutual wonder stand and stare.

Wise little one, the band below
Makes holy magic in the street.
The child above, dear frozen feet,
Recalls a Lord you ought to know.

SPENDING SPREE

"The true light, which lighteth every man that cometh into the world."
(John 1:9)

This Christmas business . . . really!
                                    Children clutching
Expensive presents in their grubby hands;
Hot tears, smeared faces, jelly in the hair,
New playthings well and truly smashed by teatime!
Too much to eat: too many close encounters
With Santa Claus in crowded High Street stores.
Too much to drink: too loud the ringing tills
And precorded bells. Can 'Silent Night' –
Relayed remorselessly from floor to floor –
Relieve your aching feet – or broken heart?
Let's close the bloated business down . . .
. . . and yet
A child was born alive in Bethlehem
Betrothing Then and There to Here and Now:
Outcast, a vagrant, narrowly escaping
Untimely liquidation by the state.
Such waifs are often seen on television.
We feel . . . or feel we ought to feel . . .
                                     Beware!
Is that the Light that Lighteth Every Man
Shining behind the cardboard Manger Scene?
And do the children feel immortal longings
Upon them as they climb the stairs to bed?
And can we build the bright Jerusalem
Among the empty beer cans? Is it true that
God, in an act so simple and so strange,
Embarked upon a spending spree of love?

181

EASTER INTERPRETED

THE EXTRA MILE?

"If a man in authority makes you go one mile, go with him two."
(Matthew 5:41)

Simon of Cyrene recalls how he was compelled to carry the cross

It serves me right.
I should have stayed away.
I needed time to pray,
Not elbow-room to contemplate the plight
Of one – two – three
Wretches condemned to prove that Rome is boss.

It serves me right.
"Done for" – the soldiers said –
"This one's as good as dead."
Grinning, they grabbed the strongest man in sight:
And that was me.
"Yes you!" they yelled – "You Jew, pick up that cross".

It serves me right.
"If someone forces you
To go a mile – go two",
Jesus had said. Strange, that an act of spite
Should set me free;
And peace be born in pain – such pain, such loss.

THE SPY AND THE GIRL

They were now approaching Jerusalem – and when he reached Bethphage and Bethany, at the Mount of Olives, he sent two of his disciples with these instructions: "Go to the village opposite, and, just as you enter, you will find tethered there a colt which no one has yet ridden. Untie it and bring it here. If anyone asks 'Why are you doing that?' say 'The Master needs it . . ." So they brought the colt to Jesus and spread their cloaks on it – and he mounted. And people carpeted the road with their cloaks, while others spread brushwood which they had cut in the fields, and those who went ahead and the others who came behind shouted 'Hosanna – Blessings on him who comes in the name of the Lord!'" (Mark 11:1-9)

The Spy:

From agent Absalom to Temple Prefect:
Blessings and Peace.
          According to instructions
I held the suspect, Jesus son of Joseph,
Closely in view throughout the day. He first
Approached the city via the Mount of Olives.
Two of his people went and fetched a colt
(Plainly by pre-arrangement). This he rode
In what one could describe as 'royal' style,
His court of ragamuffins close behind him.
Most of the gang are Galilean pilgrims;
A few from Judah. Could I recommend
Interrogation of the donkey's owner?
The crowd around him sang and shouted slogans:
"Hosanna" – this was frequently repeated:
"Blessed be the kingdom of our Father David" .
And then the one hypnotic word "Hosanna".

No one was drunk. The whole event was peaceful.
My judgement: harmless – silly – not as yet
A threat to public order. Still – of course –
Jesus of Nazareth needs closely watching.

The Girl:

Mother – listen
Don't be cross.
It's all my fault,
I'll bear the loss.

I didn't stay
To sell a thing . . .
I saw them marching,
Heard them sing;

Their song was somehow
Mixed with laughter.
I left the market,
Hurried after,

Chased the chanting
Down the street . . .
Swaying bodies,
Shuffling feet.

I raced right past them;
Got to see
The prophet-man
From Galilee.

I yelled "Hosanna"
Yelled like mad –
He turned and smiled . . .
So good – so sad.

The Spy:

The so-called prophet has a certain charm.
One cannot say the same about his twelve
Disciples: boors – the lot of them, excepting
Judas Iscariot – an able man,
Disgruntled, disillusioned, head and shoulders
Above the rest. I plan to keep in touch.
Kindly approve my claim – the standard rate
On bread and wine for entertaining Judas,
Plus cheese and dates and olives.
          Furthermore –
This may seem odd – the people took to laying
Branches on the road – and even outer
Garments.
          To keep my cover I was forced
To lay my cloak before the suspect's feet.
The ass, the man, the barefoot mob passed over.
Herewith I claim the cost of one new cloak.
All in the course of duty.
          So farewell . . .

The Girl:

My lovely veil
Was almost new,
But mother, please,
What could I do?

They all had branches –
Threw them down
To pave the prophet's
Way to town.

"Daughter of Zion" –
Someone cried
"Rejoice! Your promised
King will ride

Through David's gate
In peace!" and then
All at once
The cheering men

Laid their cloaks
Down in the dust.
No flowers! – I thought –
No palm! – I must

Give what I can –
One precious thing.
I bared my head
Before the king

And laid my veil
Right in his way.
I think: he noticed
Where it lay . . .

The colt passed by
The people trod,
Trampled it down . . .
But surely God

Will understand:
What could I do?
My lovely veil
Was almost new . . .

MR ROCK REMEMBERS

My master poured the blood-red wine;
He broke the dark brown bread.
The lamp was low: the shadows tall.
"Remember me" – he said.

"This wine I shall not drink again
Until I drink it new.
O Peter, friend, today I pray
A double prayer for you;

But Satan longs to snap you up."
I looked him in the eye.
"Let devils put the rest to flight.
Here's one who'll never fly.

My nickname stands for ever sure.
You called me, 'Mr Rock'."
The lamplight flickered: shadows moved.
He said, "Before the cock

Crows twice, you'll take a triple oath,
And swear you never knew me."
The failing flame revealed his face.
Both word and look went through me.

We left the Upper Room and went
In strange bewildered sorrow
To pray away that night of nights
To face that grim tomorrow.

The ground was damp, the wind was cold;
We heard his bitter weeping.
The wind was keen, the ground was hard:
He came, and found us sleeping.

We rubbed our wretched eyes and saw
The distant torches dancing.
We heard the traitor's muttering voice.
We saw the spears advancing.

The others ran: I swung my sword.
(Include it in your story!)
And hurt a poor conscripted slave
To save the Lord of Glory.

They gave the doom of death at night
The hiss was "Faster! Faster!"
I followed, followed, far behind
My once and future Master.

Within the cobbled court the fire
Was warm: the shadows tall.
O where was God the Father then?
I lingered by the wall.

The stones were cold: I turned my face
Towards the kindly flame.
"This man was one of them", they said.
I tasted triple shame.

Three times they flung the words – and thrice
I said I never knew
The man who called me, 'Mr Rock' .
Then – cockadoodle-doo –

The morning bird proclaimed the day,
And woke a city sleeping,
Denounced the shabby secret trial
And left poor Peter weeping.

Yet I, Disciple Number One,
Whose petty promise tumbled,
Sprang with my Lord from death to life
When bread and man were crumbled.

So let succeeding ages learn
Of Peter's pride and blunder.
And you who hear, who fear, who fall,
Take heart – and hope – and wonder.

THE WIDOW'S TALE

Once he was standing opposite the Temple treasury, watching as people dropped their money into the chest. Many rich people were giving large sums. Presently there came a poor widow who dropped in two tiny coins, which together are worth a farthing. He called his disciples to him. "I tell you this"', he said, "This poor widow has given more than any of the others – for those others who have given had more than enough, but she, with less than enough, has given all that she had to live on." (Mark 12: 42-44)

Why yes – I'm a widow. The good Lord bereft us
Of Saul when the tower of Siloam fell down.
A mason by trade sir – the work that he left us
Adorns our dear Temple and parts of the town.

As you say, I'm not wealthy – in fact we are six, sir.
Three daughters – two sons – were the work of my Saul.
The youngest is two – and a bundle of tricks, sir.
May God in His mercy be good to them all.

So my husband did well, as a man and a mason.
Our time was so busy, so sweet and so short.
But a widow must learn how to put a brave face on –
Like the lilies of stone on the garrison fort.

No no. Not his work, sir. My meagre donation?
(I noticed your Jesus – did he notice me?)
I gave my two coppers – a small celebration
To share with the Lord whose best blessings are free.

For some, as you said, sir, a lot is a little,
And a little is more than the poor can afford –
When the body is weary and patience is brittle
You shout at the children and blame the good Lord.

I'm so busy I feel more bad temper than sorrow!
But my Rachel had fever and now she can sleep,
So with oil in my lamp and fresh bread for tomorrow
I can thank the good Lord whose compassion goes deep.

And I do like your Jesus, so wise and so clever,
The smile in his arguments – always so calm:
The tales that he tells keep you thinking for ever!
He's mighty as Moses – and strong as a psalm.

My eldest is just a big lad in a hurry;
Too young and too headstrong! He does need a man
To teach him and train him. It's sometimes a worry.
But mother will do what a poor mother can.

With five to bring up, sir – by washing and sewing –
Young bodies to dress, and young faces to feed –
The children keep growing – the rent's always owing –
You don't have the time that the older ones need.

And my eldest, you know – it's an occupied city.
I wish he could learn a respectable trade.
These gangs and these groups: Dear God do have pity!
When I wake up at night I feel lost and afraid.

When the soldiers go by with their swagger and drumming
Our boys feel so bitter – but what can they do?
God spare us the great Tribulation that's coming!
I pray equal mercy for Roman and Jew.

Last year, sir, believe me, they crucified two of them:
Two mother's sons not much older than mine.
The state is quite glad to . . . do that to a few of them.
It teaches the rest not to get out of line.

When my son is out late and sleeps in half the morning,
And his face is at peace – like a three year old boy –
Then I think of those crosses, our governor's warning –
A terrible shadow creeps over my joy.

So I sent my wild Aaron to hear your good prophet.
I chose an odd day. It was "Blessed are the meek".
My villain comes back. He says "Mother, come off it –
That man said, 'If somebody strikes your left cheek

Then you must politely present him the other.
If they force you to march for a mile – then go two!
And treat Pontius Pilate like some long-lost brother.'"
Then he smiles and says "Mother, I wish it were true.

Let's give it a try." Which is why I am here, sir.
Your Jesus has got him amused and impressed.
What else can I do but hand over my fear, sir,
Give God all I've got and then hope for the best?

WHO DARES, WINS?

Dear God, it seems the good guy never wins.
Evil has come in first,
Hatred has done its worst.
The Prince of Peace has had to die
The lord of love has lost the game.
And that's the wretched end.
Yet even here, some say, new hope begins.
What if the loser won?
And Jesus who forgave and still forgives
Made mercy out of shame
Hung on the cross as king and friend
And lives – and lives –
To prove the power of love which spins the sun?

THE ALABASTER BOX

"Jesus was at Bethany, in the house of Simon the leper. As he sat at table, a woman came in carrying a small bottle of very costly perfume, pure oil of nard. She broke it open and poured the oil on his head. Some of those present said to one another angrily: 'Why this waste? The perfume might have been sold for more than three hundred pence and the money given to the poor . . .' But Jesus said, 'Let her alone . . . She has done what lay in her power. She is beforehand with anointing my body for burial . . .'" (Mark 14:3-8)

Yes sir, I broke it. Of course it was wasteful.
Plainly the company found it distasteful,
But what could I do
To silence those men all so certain they matter,
Exhausting our master with ignorant chatter?
So I pushed my way through

And perfumed his head, sir! Now there's a sensation!
A stunt by a woman of odd reputation . . .
Friend, don't you see?
Just who will the hostile contingent be blaming
For such a performance so shocking, so shaming?
Jesus – or me?

You disciples who left those good livings to follow!
Your proud protestations are thoughtless and hollow
When put to the test . . .
"Hail and Hosanna Lord! Time for a healing!
Give us a parable . . ." Jesus is reeling,
One moment of rest

Is God's gracious mercy – and that's what I gave him.
I'd spill more than luxury perfume to save him!
Who knows what I'd give!
For he was the one who awoke and unveiled me
When – too many others – had cheated and failed me . . .
So learn how to live

From Jesus, your leader. It takes no great labour
To master his message. Love God and your neighbour,
Give thanks for your bread,
Enjoy the day's beauty. Forgive all your debtors.
When you pray, say "Our Father". Be givers, not getters . . .
You know what he said.

It's as clear as cool water. And so they don't like him.
They spy on him, circle him, plot how to strike him
Down to the dust;
Those men at the top – the respectable livers,
Grave persons of property, getters not givers;
Their hate burns like lust.

Back at the feast there – you saw how he pondered
While they complained that my gift had been squandered.
"Some worthy charity
Could have been aided discreetly and quickly.
Now all we have is the sordid and sickly
Smell of vulgarity."

Three hundred pence – in their wise estimation
Wasted by me in vain search for sensation!
O what a vandal!
Destitute widows – some twenty or thirty –
Could have been favoured – but now there's a dirty
Smell of foul scandal

Rubbed onto Jesus! But my alabaster
Box of sweet perfume has honoured your master.
O yes – dear brother –
Were you like them? Did you think it the clearest
Proof of my shame, sir? That scent was the dearest
Gift of my mother.

But why did he say I had honoured his dying?
Soothed his poor flesh unaccustomed to lying
Cold under stone?
All my poor perfume proclaims his rich royalty,
Marks him the king of my heart's living loyalty!
Now he's alone –

All on his own with dear friends who don't know him.
All on his own with the critics who show him
Smiles of smooth treason.
Go back and guard him – the Lord I anointed!
Maybe I too was divinely appointed?
You know the reason

Sir, why my perfume has ruined your dinner.
You've been so kind as to talk to a sinner
Clumsily trying
To offer pure love . . . and what else is worth giving?
Care for your Jesus. All praise to his living,
Peace to his dying.

JUDAS

"Then Judas Iscariot, who was one of the twelve, went to
the Chief Priests in order to betray him . . . they were glad,
and promised to give him money . . ." (Mark 14:3-10)

Why all this waste – an alabaster flask
Broken to make a sentimental gesture?
Perfume worth a good three hundred pence!
She could have opened it and used a little.
Instead she breaks the jar and spills the lot.
It's on the floor – a messy kind of homage.
The smell in there is simply overpowering.
And now – to business, quickly . . .
                    You are here
To represent the Priests and Sacred Council
Who wish to question Jesus, son of Joseph.
I represent . . . I represent myself;
Judas Iscariot . . .
                    All right – you want
To catch the man and I can help you do it.
But hear me first: I'm not betraying Jesus;
I haven't let him down – he let me down . . .
Five thousand able-bodied men were waiting
Ready to rise: he could have been a king . . .
He sent them home with broken fish and promises . . .
(O yes, I did support the Freedom Movement:
Think what you like. I also trusted Jesus.)
He could have called the host of heaven down
To fight his country's cause . . . (He does have powers,
Uncanny powers – but greatly over-rated

I think – and not the power to see through Judas!)
His brightest gift consists in telling stories:
"Ask and you get" – I got the disappointment.
"Seek and you find" – I found the road to nowhere . . .
"Knock and the door will open" – How I knocked!
Not like the rest, dear Sir. I didn't follow
Jesus – I marched beside him, man to man.
Shoulder to shoulder – he and I – a head
Taller than all the rest . . .
                              "Dear master, please,
Explain the parable – what did you mean?"
"I'll tell you, little flock. Just gather round."
(I've got that sickly perfume on my shirt)
They never trusted me – those Galileans.
Even when we break the bread together,
Dip in the common dish, they watch – the warming
Broth defiles my mouth, my tongue, my thoughts . . .
I know they'll say I sold him for the money . . .
Just because I keep the common purse.
There's only one of them can handle coins –
Matthew: ex-tax collector. He's a crook . . .
We're wasting time. I'm not concerned with money.
I simply ask symbolic reimbursement:
Forty silver pieces, shall we say?
Twenty? Not enough! Let's make it thirty.
Agreed. Your masters will of course confirm?
Arresting Jesus? How? The stag, my friend
Will find a secret spring to drink alone.
I'll tell your priestly masters when and where:
Make sure they have the dogs to bring him down . . .

GOOD FRIDAY – THE OFFICIAL VERSION

Pontius Pilate makes his report on the crucifixion of Jesus

Your tablets ready? Take my letters.
You can revise what I dictate.
It's always wise to keep our betters
Right up to date.

"The governor-general" . . . usual stuff . . .
"From Pontius Pilate: may it please
The gods to give you health . . ." enough
Officialese.

You know the style. "We crucified,
One week ago, a local Jew."
Correction: weren't there three who died?
Yes . . . add on two.

"Three Jews were put to death. The crime:
Revolt against the Roman State.
We nail them up from time to time;
A fitting fate –

No loyalist regrets their death.
My letter deals with Number Three:
Jesus, who came from Nazareth
In Galilee.

News which I heard with some relief
At first. Not one of mine! In fact
Friend Antipas, the native chief
Refused to act.

Our local priests alleged a plot.
I thought the man a harmless crank.
For what ensued he's only got
Himself to thank.

'King of the Jews' – the name could spread
Garbled reports which might alarm.
This king could cause – alive or dead –
Minimal harm.

The title 'king' amused the crowds.
The man had called himself a king:
A king of angels, king of clouds;
That sort of thing.

A wandering prophet, not a schemer;
Convinced the world would shortly end.
Well, now the gods can tell the dreamer
What they intend.

So was the wretch deranged, insane?
Could I have found some way to save him?
Send him to Antipas again?
Flog or enslave him?

No way: that crowd was vicious, vile . . .
And while friend Jesus preached of peace
(In words, I hear, of wit and style)
The man's release

Could well have threatened public order.
I therefore gave the dogs their kill;
Though, to be frank, it was a borderline
case. But still

Duty is duty. As I said,
His teaching scarcely posed a threat
To Rome: and if it did, he's dead.
I do regret

(A private, not a public pain)
That haggard face."
          My mind's been straying.
Erase your tablets! Start again!
What was I saying?

On second thoughts – forget my letter.
Pack your writing-case and go.
The less we say of this the better.
Who needs to know?

THE SOLDIER'S STORY

"After the soldiers had crucified Jesus, they took his clothes and divided them into four parts, one part for each soldier. They also took the robe, which was made of one piece of woven cloth without any seams in it. The soldiers said to one another, 'Let's not tear it; let's throw dice to see who will get it.' This happened in order to make the scripture come true: 'They divided my clothes among themselves and gambled for my robe.'" (John 19:23-24)

The soldier who won the seamless robe of Christ has gone into a tavern. He is trying to sell the robe – or give it away . . .

Just take a look at this. My lucky day.
The dice fell right. I won the victim's robe –
Soft wool, good weave, without a single seam.
We all agreed we shouldn't rip it up.
I'm Execution Squad. We share the loot:
Sandals, loincloth, money – things like that.
It takes a man to kill a man: in fact
It takes four men to strip a man and nail
Him up to dry . . . to cry . . . to die . . .
                    Excuse
My way of speaking. No one think it's funny.
Well, some do stand and laugh – they're all civilians.
Once the cross is up a serving soldier
Never laughs . . .

            This robe – I won it fairly.
Their crooked dice, not mine.
            I'd say a woman's
Love is well and truly woven in.
His mother, sister, wife . . .
            You do feel sorry.
'King of the Jews' – they call him – what's his name?
Some Hebrew name. Look at the public notice.
He's not the man to lead a revolution
And that's for sure. We went a bit too far

Before we nailed him up. The flogging – nasty . . .
One of my partners wraps him up in purple,
Sticks a great big bird's nest on his head,
Says, "Hail, your majesty. Have pity, pity . . ."
You know, I almost thought he did have pity . . .
Him – pity us – that's odd.
               He won't take long
To die. So thank the gods for that.
               This robe:
A seamless robe of wool and mother's love . . .
There's some old woman up there, swathed in black.
Could just be her . . .
               This robe, I'd like to sell it.
Cheap and nearly new. What offers, friends?
Worn by a former king – as good as dead . . .
Speak up . . .
All right, I know I'm Execution Squad,
Jackals, vultures, call us what you like.
We spare the robe and tear the man apart.
That's it. Of course, I don't deserve an answer . . .
So what? No deal. I'll give the thing away.
You jolly folk who only want a drink
Out of sight and sound and smell of dying,
It's cool in here – was calm, before I came . . .
As for you godly folk who didn't do
A thing, kept well away and didn't laugh
At what's-his-name . . . at Jesus . . .
               Here's the robe.
Let's leave it here. So jolly folk, and godly,
Fight it out. I'm sure you know some cripple,
Beggar, madman, leper, paralytic,
In need of rags,
               That fellow Jesus knew them.

I leave the robe to you. I won it fairly.
So take a look at this . . .
               . . . Your lucky day!

AFTER GOOD FRIDAY:
THE YOUNG WOMAN'S STORY

"Suppose a woman has ten silver coins and loses one. Does she
not light a lamp, sweep the house and search diligently until she
finds it?" (Luke 15:8)

"And there were women watching from a distance who had
followed him from Galilee." (Mark 15:40)

"All I have left of him is this: a coin,
Silver, Greek – a drachma, giving glory
To some unpleasant pompous king or other –
Circled by bragging words. I never learned
To read, but as you see, I've kept the coin.
One of a set of ten. My mother's treasure.

Please, please, don't make me talk about the killing.

You know the tales he used to tell . . . a woman
Loses a precious silver coin and lights
A lamp and sweeps in every dusty cranny;
Peering, slashing cobwebs, lifting jars
And buckets, turning baskets upside down . . .
But then she finds it, whoops for sheer relief,
And calls her friends to celebrate: "At last
I've found the long-lost coin". At which those jolly
Neighbours laugh and chatter . . .

Now I've nothing:
Nothing left but this . . . a lifeless drachma.

Yes, I was there. We women stood and prayed
Until he died. I didn't look. I shut
My eyes and clutched a tiny piece of hope.

Why? Don't you see? This *is* the long-lost coin.
The very one that made the story run,
The precious silver drachma that went missing.
Most of the tales that Jesus told were true.
He didn't make them up. He *picked* them up,
Blossoming wild along the lanes of life.
How my poor mother fussed and fretted, hunted
High and low . . . until I shouted *"Look*
It's here. It's underneath my sleeping mat."
Yes, it was me. I found the famous coin.
But then, when Jesus told our tale, he left
Me out. Who cares? He turned it into simple truth;
That each and every soul is precious metal,
Dear to God, and worth a world of searching.

Before my mother died she gave this coin
To me and said, *"Most men are much the same,*
But not the man of Nazareth. He holds
The key to all the mysteries of God."

MARY MAGDALENE TELLS HER STORY

"She thought he was the gardener . . ." (John 20:15)

Don't laugh. Don't dare to laugh. I'm not a fool.
Not mad, not drunk, and least of all hysterical.
Of course I'm tired. I haven't slept at all
Since . . . Judas came and took him in the garden.
You saw it . . . you disciples – you were there;
Asleep – I'm told, but woken just in time
To see the grinning gang surrounding Jesus.
Not that it matters now . . .
                    . . . You dear disciples,
Bickering, grumbling, always in the wrong . . .
We women knew what Jesus meant, you know.
Right from the start we knew – yes, right from Galilee.
We felt him suffer – even then. He cured me,
Wrenched away the hurt, the hate, and smiled:
"Mary!" he said. It left him drained, exhausted.
I saw his eyes . . .
                    . . . That doesn't matter now.
Listen to this: Our Lord is now alive.
That's all: alive – not dead.
                    I said, "Don't laugh."
Did I say, "Sit and stare?" Or "Stand and gape?"
I haven't made it up. I'm not hysterical.
So laugh at this: I thought he was the gardener!
I asked politely: could I have the body?
"Please, sir. . . ." – I said – "Do tell me: where's the body?"
So laugh at that – you dear disciples: laugh!

Remember – back in Galilee he told us
To notice things: the hungry, cheeky, happy-
Go-lucky sparrow, sold for half a farthing:
The lilies flaming red and gold . . . to feel

God's free-for-nothing rain on face and body . . .
To smile at Solomon in all his glory;
Poor pampered king, less than a single lily!
Now listen:

All the good words from Galilee are true:
Doubly, trebly, over-and-over true!
Tried by the vicious whipping, driven home
By nail on nail, and verified in death,
In filthy death.
Proved in the sweetest prayer he ever prayed:
"Father forgive – they know not what they do!"

You know me, dear disciples – Mary Magdalene:
The shameless thing who danced for seven devils
All at once, till Jesus took the shame
And gave me back the rain, the flowers, the sparrows.

Well, he's alive . . .
                    . . . and you can take or leave it!
"Mary!"
        "My Master!"
                "Friend, you mustn't touch me!
I haven't yet ascended to my father."
That was all we said.
                I'm here to tell you.
Me! Truth beyond all telling; laughing truth!
Love . . . Light . . . The garden warm and good . . . His voice . . .
One Father . . . Yours and mine . . . One God for all . . .
So now you know. From Mary Magdalene.
Seven devils danced in my poor body;
And I'm the first to see the living Lord!
But not the last . . .
                One Father – yours and mine.
Now you can laugh. One God, for you and me.
Now you can laugh. The Lord of life is free!

REMBRANDT PAINTS
THE RISEN CHRIST

*A visitor calls on Rembrandt in his poverty-stricken old age. The
artist is painting – yet again – the scene where the risen Christ
appears to the disciples at Emmaus.*

"They knew him in the breaking of the bread." (Luke 24:35)

I thought you were the money lender, friend.
Excuse my boorishness; I am
Indeed old Rembrandt, not so long ago
Known to the cultured world of Amsterdam
For portraits, nobly done if highly priced.
My wife was a lady – did you know?
My private gallery was quite a show
In former days. Of course it had to end . . .
I also painted Jesus Christ.

From infancy I felt His spell.
I used to stand at mother's knee
And hear her tell
Me Bible stories of the blind and lame.
Those wretched woodcuts! Even then I knew
What Rembrandt, miller's son, would do:
Something simple, subtle, true –
No high baroque, no artificial game.
Both men and Master should appear the same
As our Dutch poor: like beggar boys, like me.

So I, a rising man of three-and-twenty
Tried to record Christ risen.
Talent I had in plenty;
I wanted drama, and I drew
Emmaus, where the disappointed two

Perceived Him in the breaking of the bread:
Depicting sudden dread,
Gasps and gesticulations, gaping fright,
While they, like men in prison
Longing for life and fearing death
For one eternal moment catch their breath
Before that splendid shadow ringed with light.

That picture's gone, as you'll observe –
Gone with my Eastern curios; all sold
Or pawned. But maybe I deserve
No less for being over-bold
With self, with art, with life.

And then I lost my Saskia, my wife;
Let's leave my tale untold . . .
You see, I'm still at work – same subject too:
The travellers to Emmaus, tired, depressed,
The unexpected guest;
Supper, reproaches, deep despair unspoken;
And then the moment when the bread is broken.
Kindly observe with care
My style: no straining for sensation now;
The Lord is undistinguished, shabby, plain.
(Thus old men paint who know despair,
Making a merit out of mental pain.)
They beg him to preside; the bread is blessed,
Shared: in the stillness they begin to see,
And – oh, so slowly – hope comes true.
Nothing can ever be the same again –

Not for them and not for me.
They recognise the living Lord. See, there!
There, in my art! 0 how
Can language cope? Don't let me paint in vain.
Perceive Him, friend. I put Him there for you.

THE ICON-PAINTER TELLS HIS STORY

Andrey Ryublov is the most famous of Russian icon-painters. Here
he tells his story to a group of visitors. The poem is based on the
film of Ryublov's life by Andrey Tarkovsky.

So did you come to see me paint?
Lord, save a soul from fame!
Or did you want to hear a tale
Of scandal, sin and shame?

This picture, sir? It's not for sale.
I'm glad your little boy
Likes it. For him, if not for you,
I'll tell you. Children's joy

Is life and peace to old Andrey
Who loved the solemn singing
Long ago; the icons framed
In gold; the mass-bell ringing;

And loved the Virgin best of all,
Set in her jewelled frame,
But feared the Christ who comes to judge
With eyes of piercing flame.

"Mother of God", I prayed, when twelve
St Andrew's Days had run –
She left the frame and touched my hand
And whispered: "Paint my Son,

In churches through the Russian lands
For souls who cannot read.
Show them a Lord who comes to help
In pain and fear and need."

I left the church and walked alone
Beside my secret stream.
I stopped where silver birches quiver.
There I dreamed my dream –

208

Or was it truth? The branches shook;
A ragged peasant boy
Swung to the ground and touched my hand
And said: "I wish you joy:

Andrey, the monk-to-be, the man
Of prayer, shall spend his youth
Learning, while others gape and stare,
To paint the inward truth."

The birches moved. The boy – who else
But Christ? – was gone; I laughed
The seven long years it took to learn
The icon-painter's craft.

I showed the Christ in Mary's arms
With eyes of loving flame,
Helping to heal the Russian lands
Until the Tartars came

With fires that watched us night by night
Around our walls until
They smashed the city gate and rushed
To rob and rape and kill.

That shrieking girl! I saw her eyes
Ablaze with fear and pain.
My hand, that drew the Virgin's son,
Shattered a human brain.

We hid the Tartar's corpse; the girl
Ran off with one of ours.
I walked alone through endless woods
And heard uncanny powers

Whisper through the marching pines:
"Thou shalt not paint again.
The monk who dips his hand in blood
Is cursed." I said, "Amen!"

And wandered through the Russian lands
For seven long years' disgrace.
One image only filled my mind:
The Tartar's gaping face.

Our churches rose again. They said:
"Monk, you must come and paint."
I left their walls blank as my mind.
I prayed no prayer. No saint

Smiled in my dream: the Virgin stood
Cold in the icon's frame.
The Russian fields and woods were dumb.
The bells clang-clanged my shame;

Until I came at last to find
My secret stream and felt
The silver birches shiver. "Lord,"
I mumbled as I knelt –

Hearing a voice unheard, perceiving
Someone I could not see –
"Once before you met me here.
Have you no hope for me

Who learned the icon-painter's art
Through long and hungry years?
I drew your face. I struck and killed.
I bore the pain. My tears

Have never moved your mother standing
Still where I set her, high
Above the smoking lamps of faith.
Lord, let me paint or die!"

The restless leaves replied. My secret
Stream moved slowly on.
I felt the wind. My head no longer
Ached. The One had gone.

So had my guilt – the guilt of blood.
"The monk is not too old,"
I said, and smiled at Russian lands
Renewed in green and gold.

This icon – no, it can't be bought –
Is painted by the book.
The folding Virgin's veil,
The hands, the tender look,

Are all laid down in ancient laws,
Prescribed, I think, by Greeks.
These, as a humble monk, I keep:
Since God in glory speaks

Even in my poor painter's art
Through human hands and eyes.
The Virgin's son appears – as rules
Require – both young and wise.

And yet – this Christ is mine alone.
True with the truth I know.
He might surprise you by a stream
Where silver birches grow.

QUESTIONING SIMON

Where have you been, Brother Simon from Africa?
Nobody saw you for many a day!
"Once in a lifetime I went to Jerusalem –
Off to the city to wonder and pray."

Was it so marvellous, Simon the Traveller?
What was the best of the sights you could see?
"God's holy temple all golden and glittering
Crowded with pilgrims as happy as me."

Were there bad trips, Mr Simon the Happy Man?
Something disgusting? We dare you to tell!
"Gaping at Jesus, the friend of the friendless,
Hounded along till he stumbled and fell."

Surely you helped, Master Simon the Strong Man?
Gave him encouragement – do tell us how.
"Not till the soldiers came running and yelling:
'Pick up that cross, man, and pick it up now!'"

Where did they take you, poor Simon the Prisoner?
You with the burden – the Man by your side?
"Grimly to Calvary – there they got rid of me.
Jesus was hung on the cross till he died."

Was there a miracle, Simon the Sufferer?
Something amazing and hopeful and true?
"Yes, when he prayed for the people who hated him:
'Father forgive, they don't know what they do.'"

Why say 'Good Friday', Sir Simon the Simpleton ?
Didn't he perish in squalor and shame?
"Jesus was Man of the Match with King Cruelty:
Living and loving – he's Lord of the game."

A HANDFUL OF HYMNS

A HYMN FOR A CHURCH ANNIVERSARY

Lord of ages long forgotten,
Still sustaining time and space,
Once again we offer praises
Gathered in this hallowed place.
Faithful saints appear as shadows,
Flickering memories from the past;
Yet we trust they live in glory;
Endless mercy holds them fast.

While we celebrate the present,
Recollect the busy year,
May the Christ of hidden glory
Always find a welcome here.
Here let happy prayer be offered,
Haunting fears be cast away,
Friendships made and sins forgiven:
Father, bless our solemn day.

Now we turn to face the future
– Joy or grief, not ours to know –
May the Prince of Peace walk with us,
Show us where we ought to go.
Let the doors of love stand open,
While we play our willing part.
Jesus reigns today, for ever,
King of every Christian heart.

IN PRAISE OF CHRIST THE KING

How fearsome and far
The universe runs!
Who counts every star?
Who numbers new suns?
But Christ is the king
Of unthinkable space;
So stand up and sing
Of his goodness and grace.

Strange secrets of life
New knowledge can tell.
Amazing the strife
Of microbe and cell!
Yet Christ is the friend
Of the tiniest flower.
Rejoice without end
In his goodness and power.

The last and the least
Our Jesus calls best,
Proclaiming the feast
His Father has blessed.
To ruin and shame him
They nail him up high,
But now we acclaim him
For daring to die.

That sorrow is past:
Let wrong do its worst.
He'll reign at the last
Who ruled at the first –
The Lord of all years
That are coming to birth,
As laughter and tears
Grow together on earth.

Then go, sister, go,
And pray, brother pray:
Let everyone know
The Christ of today.
His truth sets us free:
(How the story rings true!)
He conquered for me;
And he's calling for you.

A PENTECOST HYMN

We praise you, Lord of love,
Whose Holy Spirit came,
Amazing, like a flame,
Enchanting as a dove.
At Pentecost your people knew
That mighty presence, strange yet true.

Our Lord, so long ago
Was bold in deed and word
And still his call is heard.
His friendship we can know.
Your Spirit plays a lively part,
Revealing him to mind and heart.

For like the wind that drives
The racing clouds along,
His mercy, wise and strong,
Sustains our busy lives.
Great God of Pentecost, we pray,
Give strength for ever – and today.

A HYMN FOR A RETIREMENT

"Well done, good and faithful servant" — *Matthew 25:21*

Great God of love and grace,
Whose fearsome power extends
Beyond all time and space,
We dare to call you friends.
For each and every one you call
With "follow me" to one and all.

Your service teaches truth
And makes us free indeed.
Help us, in age or youth,
To meet our neighbour's need:
And may our gentle Saviour still
Give strength to know and do Your will.

On this thanksgiving day,
Which marks a race well run,
Your people meet to say
 "Dear friend(s) in faith, well done!
Your Master knows the busy years
Lived out in joy and toil and tears."

We promise here and now
To serve our whole life long.
Accept the solemn vow
We make in prayer and song.
Dear Lord, the past is truly blessed:
Let future ventures be the best.

PSALM 8: A NEW PARAPHRASE

"O Lord our Lord, how majestic is your name in all the earth!"

Great God of love, we gaze
On vast and fearsome skies.
And hear your happy praise
Extolled in infants' cries.
Your ageless might the hills proclaim
And now we dare to bless your name.

Your majesty is shown
As moon and stars give light,
And galaxies unknown
Proclaim your fearful might.
And yet your mercy never ends:
Your Son – our Saviour – calls us friends.

On earth, where life began
You gave us strength and skill
To think and shape and plan
And work for good and ill:
With knowledge, careless greed and power
To injure bird and beast and flower.

Then grant us time to mend
Your world too quickly torn,
Let joyful truth extend
To children yet unborn.
O Lord, for evermore the same,
How great and glorious is your name.

A HARVEST HYMN

Great God of all seasons, in mercy and power
You rule every star and rejoice in each flower;
Once more for good harvest we offer our praise,
And promise to give you the fruit of our days.

For autumn proclaims You, in russet and gold,
And winter obeys You, with keen cutting cold.
Till spring with new greenness takes all by surprise,
And summer brings fullness to gladden our eyes.

Through fields full of plenty the harvesters go,
While others must labour with sickle and hoe.
And some are kept hungry by folly and greed:
Lord, help us remember our neighbour in need.

Through skill and through science our harvests increase.
Let knowledge be used to bring plenty and peace,
To free the world's poor from the terrors of dearth:
Lord, help us to cherish your bountiful earth.

In wonder and faith, on this truth we rely:
Your goodness and wisdom will never run dry.
The best of our hearts and our gardens we bring
To crown you, dear Lord, as our Friend and our king.

THE COUNTRY-AND-WESTERN
COWBOY CAROL

Caesar Augustus
The Sheriff of Rome
Drove poor Mary
Away from home,

Made sad Herod
A Big Bad Ranger.
He hired hitmen
To blow away danger.

Mr Anonymous
Ran the saloon.
Left poor Joseph
To gaze at the moon.

Caesar and Herod
And Mr Anon
Hadn't a clue
What was going on.

"Where's that Prince
Of Peace? Let's go!"
Low-down shepherds
Were in the know.

"Across the farmyard.
See that shed?
One small candle . . .
Mind your head . . .

Drop your weapons!
Now kneel down.
The Lord of Life
Has come to town.

He don't need
No badge or gun,
And he shall reign
While rivers run."

Little Lawman
Lurking here:
You shall be the Lord
Of the wild frontier.

219

A LULLABY

(to a melody by Thomas Campion)

Jesus child, we welcome you,
Lord of life when time began.
By your birth – so strange so true –
God has given all He can.

Loving heart and voice reply
With a simple lullaby.

You have come to bring us life:
Make us happy, make us one.
Put an end to toil and strife
In a Christmas well begun.

Loving heart and voice reply
With a simple lullaby.

May my foe become my friend.
Anger, sleep, resentment cease.
By your crib let troubles end:
You have come to bring us peace.

Loving heart and voice reply
With a simple lullaby.

AN OFFERING OF PRAYER

THE SEVEN AGES OF PRAYER

"One man in his time plays many parts;
His acts being seven ages . . ." (Shakespeare)

The first age: the infant

God bless Grandpa, God bless Nan,
Help me do the best I can.
God bless Dad – and God bless Mum.
Please, please, please make Santa come.

The second age: the schoolboy

God, our team has got to win . . .
Make this corner-kick go in!
Sorry if this prayer's a sin.
Some of them are praying too . . .
Lord, I leave it up to you.

The third age: the lover

Fragile Lord of Life, asleep in a haybox,
All I can offer is bitterness, rage and despair.
We were a Holy Family once – or I thought so.
Now I'm a Solo Carer – left in the lurch.
Witchcraft doesn't work – or I'd certainly jinx him . . .
Damn . . . My darling baby is starting to yell.
Let me offload the pain, Lord, just for a moment.
Otherwise how could I ever hope to forgive?

The fourth age: the soldier

'Peacekeepers' – that's the new label:
'Pigs in the middle' – I'd say:
Christ, as you sleep in your stable
I'll be patrolling all day.

Some we protect don't respect us
Some are intending to kill.
You're into Peace – so protect us:
Top us all up with Goodwill.

Last year, Your day was a beauty.
Nobody ended up dead.
Guess what I need when on duty?
Eyes in the back of my head!

The fifth age: the judge

Background reports are several inches thick.
I've read them all with close attention, Lord . . .
Plus learned Counsel's Pleas on either side.
And now to play the part for which You picked me:
Judging.
Since prayer is honest thinking in Your presence,
I turn my thoughts to him, and what he did
To them . . .
I also think of me, and what You do
For me . . .
And ask that this poor fool – a man like him –
May for a while be well-informed and wise.
With reasons running steady, clear and cool.
Amen.
That's it: and now . . . to read the file again.

The sixth age: the widow

This is the path. The air was warm and still,
But now the roaring motorway runs by.
Before he even put the question I
Answered, "Of course I will."

Your mercy gave us forty years together,
Sharing the joys and pains of board and bed;
So when we knew for certain he was dead
I struggled in the tether

Of choking grief. But now I go on living
Learning to walk our secret Lovers' Way
Once more – and find the stubborn heart to pray
In silent sad thanksgiving.

The seventh age: in the nursing home

Who was that?

I don't recall the face.

Why the red hat?

What is this place?

Why am I here?

Why don't they let me go

Home to mum . . . ? She has a proper tree

With candles – not that silly thing

Over there . . . She's knitting gloves for me . . .

My mum can sing . . .

Better than them . . . I know

Those words . . . Be near me Lord, be near . . .

A PRAYER FOR NUCLEAR DISARMAMENT

The first atom bomb – dropped on Hiroshima – was called 'Little Boy'

They called you 'Little Boy'.
How strange a name.
To give a bomb that scattered so much pain
And left so many thousands dead;
And since you came
Our lives can never be the same;
You taught us to destroy
Our world – and left a looming cloud of dread –
Strange 'Little Boy'.

And now the world is full of 'Little Boys'
Atomic bombs that make no noise,
But seem to sleep
In dungeons underground; or creep
In submarines beneath the deep
And restless sea.
The Bomb is here to stay.
What magic spell can make it go away
And set us human beings free?

Great God of every race and creed:
Give us the faith and commonsense we need
To hold a steady hand
Of friendship out;
And learn to understand
Our foreign partner's pain and doubt.
Help us dismantle bombs and fears.
Then little girls and boys –
And grown-ups too –
In every land
Through coming years
Shall learn to share their tears and joys.

Lord, may this dream come true.

AN ATTEMPT AT PRAYER

Before the Icon of our Lady of Tenderness

"Come unto me, you weary one,
And I will give you rest."
Great God! The game has only just begun.
See how the Word aspires to think and speak,
Laying his wistful face on mother's cheek,
His fragile arm across her breast.

"My yoke is easy and my burden light."
Well, yes and no.
Maternal pain
Is well and truly done,
But Mary's grief of mind has far to go
In who-knows-what distress,
Stumbling through hidden hate and open spite.

"So come and learn: my yoke will set you free."
Good God! The answer's "yes".
Expanding universe, take this from me:
Thanks to her unassuming Son
The game of grace is well and wisely won.
Love has the last and happy laugh:
The timeless words ring true.
Therefore, on mine and all the world's behalf,
Dear Lord, I say – and pray – them back to you.

SHALL I RISK IT?

Dear God, suppose I go
An extra mile
To help my foe:
Will scowling fear dissolve into a smile?
I just don't know!
And if I try to lift
The load of those who seem
To hide a bitter heart,
Will they accept my gift,
Suspect a spy
Or greet a friend?
Will hatred ever really end?
Is making peace a crazy dream?
Someone, sometime, simply has to try!
Give me the courage, Lord, to make a start.

CHOICES

How can we know
Which way to go?
When to say "yes"?
When to say "no"?
We're young: we'd like to try
Our wings and fly
Happy and high.

Dear God, please give us all,
Courage and commonsense and skill
To love the truth and spot the lie.
Don't let us fall
For crooked talk and phony fun,
For then your loving will
Is gladly done.

A PRAYER BEFORE THE ICON OF THE VIRGIN AND CHILD 'SHOWING THE WAY'

"Show us the way,
Young Lord, we pray."
"Freely you get, so freely give!
My words direct you: read, obey . . . and live."

"How can we know
Which way to go
When hope grows cold and fears lie deep?"
"I am the shepherd boy who loves the sheep."

"How will it end?
And where?" *"Look, friend . . .*
The lilies neither toil nor spin.
I am the Way. You see? Shall we begin?"

NOVEMBER CAROL

Lord of the drizzle, the damp and the chill;
Lord of the leaves that lie soaking and still;
Christmas comes earlier, year after year.
Santa's been sighted! Your season is here.

TV commercials proclaim the good news;
Make us an offer we dare not refuse.
Come with your credit cards: stand up and spend!
Pay when the universe comes to an end.

Lord of November, come early, come soon.
Gleam through the mist of our grey afternoon.
Short and depressing and dull is our day.
Come with the catalogues: come Lord – and stay.

A PRAYER FOR CHRISTMAS EVE

Lord, you were with us here
Throughout the anxious year
Not far away –
Though fractious fear and doubt
Conspired to turn you out:
Through every hasty, hurrying day
You stood your ground – unseen, yet always near.

Soon we shall say
Unlikely King, come in!
On Christmas Eve we wait
To celebrate
The Word made new-born flesh . . . and bone and skin.
Young Prince of Peace, you have a world to win.

Mysterious God, you live
Beyond our dearest dreams – our deepest thought:
And yet we glimpse you in a human face.
Come, Lord, to grace
Our humdrum here and now, and give
Wisdom to work and wonder as we ought . . .
. . . Welcome to this holy, happy place.

A PRAYER FOR LENT
AND SPRINGTIME

Lord of green and growing spring –
Whose gentle power
Waylays us in an unexpected flower –
Today we bring
Garlands of mingled hope and fear;
But You are here,
Though fears prevail and hopes are few:
God of springtime, make us new.

Christ of sad and solemn Lent
We watch You go
Towards a cruel trial whose end we know;
And so present
New wreaths of joy to crown Your pain:
For You will reign.
Such is our faith – so strangely true:
God of springtime, make us new.

Almighty Victor, Easter King –
Who played and won,
And proved that love sustains the stars and sun –
We dare to bring
Our fragile lives for grace to fill
With glad goodwill;
And speak, in simplest love, with You.
God of springtime, make us new.

TRANSLATIONS

A SONNET IN EXILE

"France, mère des arts . . . "

by Joachim du Bellay (1522-1560)
from 'Les Regrets' (1558)

The arts of peace and war declare your fame,
Dear mother France, who nursed me at the breast.
But now I wander like a lamb distressed:
Lost among woods and caves I cry your name.
You owned me as your child, so tell me why
No answer comes. In grief I call again.
Dear cruel France, surely you know my pain . . .
Only poor Echo mocks me in reply.

Fierce wolves are prowling on the field of death.
Winter is near, I feel his icy breath
Touch me. My timid skin recoils in shock.
Your other lambs have grazing to content them,
Where neither wind nor wolf nor cold torment them.
But I remain – the straggler of the flock.

MICHELANGELO

Translated from the German of C.F. Meyer

Midnight. A single glimmering flame: no sound.
The tall old man is Michelangelo,
His children – pallid marble – stand around.
His thoughts run deep: but time is moving slow.
Silence: the cunning hammer lies at rest:
For now the sculptor wrestles with the Word . . .
Is Dante's ghost the subject of his quest?
Shall Wisdom out of Holy Writ be heard?
Farewell to Raphael – his day is done.
For beauty's gracious blossoms faded fast
And now the leaves which flutter, one by one . . .
Speak of Eternity, of pleasure past . . .
The Master's face is strange and solemn . . . Look . . .
At last he seems to speak: is someone there?
Slowly the sculptor sets aside the book
And whispers to the dark and empty air:
'Those Fantasies were sweet – they stole away
The time I should have spent on seeking you.
I shake my aged head - but still they say
"Trust us – You King of Art – our tales were true . . ."
I should have grasped your Self – the inmost truth:
A dazzling robe was all that I could see:
The power of Beauty overwhelmed my youth;
Now Righteousness has little time for me –
Grown grey in guilt – and doubly strong in error
What hope of heaven now? What claim on grace?
What can I offer now but slavish terror,
A thirsty soul that longs to see your face?
I twist and turn: but who will set me free?
My sullen heart is hardened. You alone
Great God, can make a masterpiece of me,
Tearing your image from the lifeless stone.

Let splinters fly and fall. Lay blow on blow.
Sculptor, arise: with equal skill and might,
Wielding the hammer well – to shape and show
The Form, divinely true, revealed in light . . .

A PRAYER

Translated from the German of Eduard Mörike

Of pain and of pleasure,
Lord – send what you will.
Your judgements are right
And I trust in you still.
Yet this I request:
No surplus of sorrow
Or even delight.
With both in due measure
My heart is at rest.

TWO GREEK EPIGRAMS

The Aphrodite of Cnidos

(in Greek metre)

"Shame" said the goddess of love – at the sight of her statue.
  "When did Praxiteles see me – nude and alone?"

Heliodora's all night party

(in English metre)

"The garland fades upon my lady's brow.
Her smile provides a brighter garland now."

THE LAND OF CANAAN

Translated from the Russian of Elizaveta Kuzmin-Karavaeva

This poem – and the one which follows – were written in France, during the 1930s. The writer, a Russian in exile, had become a nun in the Orthodox Church. In the Soviet Union the attack on religious faith was at its height and the communist revolution was beginning to devour its children. As 'Mother Maria', the author was to die a martyr's death in Ravensbruck concentration camp.

Honey and milk were over there:
Juice of the grape was free for taking:
Here – ruin, fear, remorse, despair:
Snow on the fields – a body aching.
For me a blessed fate is planned
As madness tears the truth apart –
O Russia, wretched Promised Land,
Your every inch commands my heart.
Face to the dust I lie alone,
With arid clay my spirit blending.
Handfuls of sand and splintered stone
Mingle to make one flesh . . . unending . . .

"I CHOOSE THE GREENWOOD NOW . . ."

I choose the greenwood now; poor peace is there;
Gravel and sand, earth, wood obey your will:
From dust you build a secret house of prayer,
A world where matins may be chanted still.
Slowly, so slowly see the domes arise,
Nameless, unearthly – dare we still detect
A Presence? Here alone – O strange surprise!
You stand revealed as mighty Architect.
Against the men of sin you raise your rod:
They fall and die – defeated, dark, inglorious.
And what am I? A single brick: Lord God,
Take me and build, Designer all-victorious.

ENCOUNTER WITH PUSHKIN

Alexander Pushkin (1799 – 1836) is Russia's greatest poet. This selection of translations – first published in 'The Complete Works of Alexander Pushkin' in English (Milner and Co., 2000) – illustrates various aspects of his achievement.

Young Pushkin

Pushkin's poetic talents were recognised while he was still a schoolboy at the prestigious Lycée near St Petersburg

LAIS DEDICATES HER MIRROR TO APHRODITE

Here is my mirror, dear queen, to delight you,
Goddess of beauty, for ever resplendent!
Fear of grey sorrow shall never affright you,
Lady immortal, transcendent.
But I, poor slave to destiny – must fear
Within the mirror's depths to see
The one who haunts me here –
The one who used to be.

Lais was a celebrated Greek courtesan

TO MY COMRADES ON LEAVING THE LYCEE AT TSARSKOYE SELO

*Former pupils were expected to serve the Tsar by joining
the Army or the Civil Service. Pushkin explains
that he has no intention of doing either!*

Gone are the years of isolation!
The time has come to say farewell —
To fields of fun and education:
The novice leaves his lonely cell.
We part — but golden days are coming;
The ways divide, but hopes are bright.
We hear the world's insistent humming
And take the road in high delight.
One lad becomes a soldier bold;
A shako hides that mighty brain!
He learns to swing the sabre well
But dawn parade is deadly cold;
He's frozen stiff — perhaps a spell
On guard will thaw him out again.
The next finds thoughts of honour funny,
And much prefers the Honours List.
Of noble birth, he bows to Money,
Learning to creep and crawl and twist;
While I, the Eldest Son of Sloth,
Too calm to fret, too wise to creep,
Accepting fate's decrees — am loth
To leave my private world of sleep.
Hussars and scribes are all the same;
Shakos and quills disgust my soul:
Why should I play the army game
Or climb the Civil Service pole?
Lay off! Respect the way I feel!

Dear friends, I don the daring Cap
Of Liberty – till some mishap
Makes me put on a casque of steel.
So watch this idle fellow walk
At ease beneath the summer sun,
Unmoved by disapproving talk,
With waistcoat buttons left undone.

TO KÜCHELBECKER

*Wilhelm Küchelbecker (1793 – 1846), a romantic poet, was one
of Pushkin's schoolmates and lifelong friends*

These final words – in distant loneliness –
I write for you, companion of my heart.
Ye gods that guard our schooldays, bless
This happy fellowship – now torn apart!
Too soon the years of brotherhood have flown;
Our league of loyal friends will meet no more.
Farewell! May heaven's protection follow
The path you take! May great Apollo
And smiling Fortune go before!
May love be yours – yes, love – to me unknown:
Warm love, with hopes, and raptures and delights
To speed your life – like some enchanted dream –
And bless your days and soothe your peaceful nights.
Farewell! In days to come, perhaps through fire and fear,
Or wandering safe at home beside a murmuring stream,
I vow to hold our friendship fast.
Lastly I pray – and hope that Destiny will hear –
Let each and every friend find happiness at last!

ARION

In 1824 Pushkin found himself on the fringes of the Decembrist Conspiracy – an early attempt to overthrow Tsar Nicholas. In the poem ARION he compares himself to a Greek minstrel of legend, who was thrown overboard by superstitious sailors, but carried to safety on a dolphin's back. It seems that the wives and widows of the Decembrists, languishing in Siberian exile, were not entertained.

The boat was full. We sped along.
Some set the sails and hauled the ropes.
The gallant oarsmen made their mark:
We faced the deep with highest hopes.
Our helmsman – silent, wise and strong –
Guided the overloaded bark.
I too was there – enraptured, I
Sang to the lads. Then came the shock.
A sudden whirlwind struck the sea.
Captain and crew will sail no more.
Only the mystic bard – that's me –
Survived the storm to reach the shore.
Leaving my singing robe to dry,
Draped on a warm and sunlit rock,
I chant my anthems – as before.

The 'helmsman' and 'captain' is the Decembrist leader Colonel Pestel, who was hanged. Küchelbecker was sent into exile.

Pushkin the Poet of Love

THE DESIRE FOR FAME

When tenderest love had laid me captive at your feet.
Remember dear? My wordless rapture was complete.
"Yes, you are mine!" I thought – your eyes were warm and kind!
How could a futile dream of glory cross my mind?
The vain and giddy world had chased me far away:
The poet's calling seemed absurd and childish play.
Wearied by endless storms, why should I ever miss
The tedious buzz of praise, or blame's resentful hiss?
Did rumour's graceless verdicts cloud my spirit then?
You laid your gentle hand upon my head again.
Those eyes were full of longing: gently bending near
You whispered "Do you love me? Are you happy, dear?
Promise you won't forget me . . . tell me you will never
Leave me for someone else . . . our joy must last for ever . . ."
My happy heart stood still; bereft of speech, I caught
My breath. In pure delight, I never even thought
That other days could come . . . the fearful time to part;
But now – what can I say? The pain, the broken heart,
Betrayal, slander, torment, tears and bitter shame
Are heaped on me, and I am left to bear the blame.
Like some unhappy soul, when lightning strikes beside him,
At dusk, alone, without a light to guide him.
Enough! For now new longing sets my soul on fire:
The thought of public fame awakens strong desire . . .
The praise of many mouths will often bring us near;
For when the world applauds, you too are bound to hear,
Then, when my famous name is ringing all around,
You will recall another, truer sweeter sound:
In darkness in the garden, sad and broken hearted.
I made my final plea – remember? – as we parted.

SEPARATION

Pushkin loved often – and deeply

Farewell to joy! I heard the fatal knell.
Waking in tears beside the dark abyss
I turned – in trembling fearfulness – to kiss
Your hand once more . . . and nevermore . . . Too well
The memory lives! My heart was full of dread.
Wrestling with pain unspeakable, I said:
"Some joys will still remain, although we part,
As memories fade, our dreams will ease the grief.
Gloomy despair can never crush the heart
Or shake the hermit in his lonely cell.
Surely the passing days will bring relief,
The kindly Muse present harmonious aid . . .
Friendship will do its gentle best, as well . . .
And so the night that clouds the soul will fade."
Little I knew of love. My grief goes on.
Little I knew the heart . . . the hours crawl past . . .
The dreary days go by: my joys are gone;
Where is the soothing drug that says "Forget"?
Dear friend, your tender presence haunts me yet,
But gloom and disillusion hold me fast.
When daylight dawns upon the looming hill
I long for you, desire your beauty still . . .

Night falls – the moon of autumn rises – then
I fall asleep, to dream – and dream again.
My fitful slumber teems with thoughts of you.
I speak your name – as if against my will.
Listen! Your voice! If only that were true . . .
Lost in the noisy crowd, alone, unblinking.
I sit confused. My eyes are blank. I stare
At friends, and scorn their foolish chatter, thinking:
"Detect my chilly secret if you dare."
Even the Lyre – my comfort – cannot please
The ailing soul. That ever-plangent strain
Grows heavy, dull and sad. It cannot ease
My grief, for thoughts of parted love remain.
Let us be joined in longing, you and I!
Sweet friend, when all your artless songs portray
My distant loneliness and present pain,
Maidens will hear the mournful chords you play
And pause awhile, and think – and spare a sigh.

O LET ME, DEAREST, BARE MY SOUL BEFORE YOU

O let me, dearest, bare my soul before you,
And find delight in friendship, true and tried.
For life has laid me low . . . I now implore you
To let me rest contented by your side.
Do you recall the early days, dear heart?
Young lad, young lass, we learned the body's art . . .
So soon made one . . .

            . . . too soon to part . . .

Sadly I lived and little joy I tasted
In foreign lands adrift beyond befriending . . .
An aimless life was well and truly wasted
In wretched boredom, emptiness unending.

Why do I live – when happiness is dust?
For fun and friendship I was never born!
You know the rest – forsaken, proud, forlorn,
Coldly I drank the bitter cup of lust.

(left unfinished)

NO REGRETS

No, no. Regrets will never do.
Our days, dear friends, are on the run
Like mist before the morning sun;
The stream of time cascades downhill –
But nothing shakes my love for you . . .
Was there a plan, or just a whim
By which the fates decreed to fill
Life's chalice – far from empty still?
With tingling lips we touch the brim –
Gulping delights in full profusion:
Hope, loving, ecstasy at last . . .
And then as always . . .
                              Disillusion . . .

We blossom, yes . . . our joys run deep . . .
But jaded memory stands aghast:
And still the heart cries out for sleep,
Yearning for peace in pleasures past.

(left unfinished)

Versatile Pushkin

HELIOS, LORD OF THE SUN

Pushkin was a virtuoso in the use of metre. This translation from the French poet André Chénier is written in classical hexameters.

"Helios, Lord of the sun, with the bow of sonorous silver!
God of Claros, attend! Accept the prayer of an aged
Sightless soul who will surely perish unless you protect him!"
Thus did the blind man speak, and sat on a boulder, exhausted . . .
Shepherds who kept their flocks – three sons of a desolate landscape –
Warned by barking dogs, set off to follow, and quickly
Found him, frail and alone. They deplored his pitiful weakness;
Heeded his prayer, drew near, and listened, wondering: "Is this
Old man really a god? White-haired and blind and forsaken –
Tall and strangely proud, with a simple lyre at his girdle?
When he speaks he commands high heaven, and rouses the waters!"
Now the unhappy pilgrim heard their footsteps approaching;
Offered an anxious hand . . . "Take heart," they told him, "and tell us
Is there a god concealed within that withering body?
He who guards our Greece?" (for thus they spoke to the stranger)
"Surely your age is adorned with truly magnificent splendour!
Should you be mortal man – then know that the merciful waters
Cast your lot with friends . . ."

THE BARON'S RETURN

*While in exile, in the far south of Russia, Pushkin met the
banished Polish poet Adam Mickiewicz. He adapted and
translated the latter's powerful tale 'The Ambush'.*

Late at night a lord comes riding . . .
Watch him, through the castle striding:
(See the servants shake with dread)
First, the bedroom . . . well-suspected! –
Next, the curtains – as expected –
No one there: an empty bed!

See him now, with eyes half-closing
Spend his thoughts in dark supposing . . .
Twirl his grey moustache, and then
(Lord of Poland's plains, victorious,
Wise in love, in battle glorious)
Bellow, "Are you dogs or men?

"You – my serf – suggest a reason
Why the door stands wide – what treason
Chained the watchdogs? . . . Stupid brute!
Bring a musket, knife and fetters;
Did we try to fool our betters?
Let me teach you how to shoot . . ."

Lord and lad go scouting, keeping
Stealthy lookout, slowly creeping
Through the trees at dead of night.
In the grove, despising danger,
Stands a young unhappy stranger;
Sits a lady dressed in white.

Now he whispers: "All are perished:
All the hopes I vainly cherished,
All the happiness I sought . . .
Tender touch of gentle fingers,
(How the sad remembrance lingers!)
Lost at last, betrayed and bought.

"Through the years I wooed you plainly,
Through the years I served you vainly:
All my yearning passed you by:
Did the baron's heart lie bleeding?
Silver coins came loudly pleading.
You accepted. Tell me why . . .

"Through the night your squire has ridden,
Ever faithful, still unbidden,
All to kiss your tender hand . . .
May my sorrows touch you never!
Soon I say farewell for ever.
Soon I seek a foreign land."

While he kneels before her, sighing;
Hears her long and bitter crying,
Lurking spies prepare the gun:
Pour the powder – killing's fuel –
Load the bullet – round and cruel –
Ramrod home! – a job well done.

"Master, please, why did you choose me . . . ?
I'm a wretched shot – excuse me . . ."
(This is all the serf could say)
"Eyes are stinging – hands are shaking:
What a noise the wind is making . . .
Half the powder's blown away."

"Quiet, you whining fool. Tomorrow
Be prepared for pain and sorrow.
Check the powder: take your aim . . .
Left a little . . . see that beauty?
Higher . . . kill her. Do your duty.
Leave the other . . . he's my game."

Then a sudden shot resounded.
Both the lovers stood dumbfounded;
Someone shrieked and fell down dead.
Yes, the lad was primed and ready,
Held the musket straight and steady,
Shot his master through the head.

THE TWA CORBIES

In 1828 Pushkin published an adapted version of the ballad, 'The Twa Corbies' ('As I was walking all alane'). His poem is retranslated into Border Scots, using the Russian poet's chosen metre.

See the hungry corbie fly.
See the greedy corbie cry,
"Brither, brither, can ee say
Whaur we twae will dine the day?"

Brither corbie croaks again:
"Whaur's the flesh? Fu' weel I ken.
By the cairn, across the plain
Lies a noble laddie slain.

Whae's the killer – and for whit?
Three there are that mind it yit.
Three tae tell whae did the deed:
Mistress, falcon, sable steed.

High the haughty foeman rides.
Deep i' the wuds the falcon bides.
Div ee think the lassie's greetin'?
A' she wants is . . . lover's meetin'."

THE PILGRIM

Pushkin's wide interests – and great versatility – are on display in this adaptation of the beginning of John Bunyan's 'Pilgrim's Progress'

One day I wandered through a dreary dale
When suddenly my heart began to fail.
A heavy burden made me gasp for breath,
As when some murderer hears the doom of death.

I bowed my head, I wrung my hands in grief;
My soul cried out – in pain beyond relief –
Sobbing and moaning, racked with feverish fear:
"What shall I do? Where flee? For surely doom is near!"

Lamenting thus, I hurried home again;
No one could understand my inner pain.
I spoke but little – watched the children play –
And tried to hide my gloomy thoughts away;
But hour by hour I felt the pain increase
Until my breaking heart refused to hold its peace.

"Woe to us all! Dear children! Darling wife!"
I cried. "Know this! My soul is full of strife
And fear! A grievous burden weighs me down:
The hour is close at hand: unhappy town!
Too soon in roaring flame shall all be burned!
Through fire and wind to dust and ashes turned . . .
And all are doomed to perish in a day
Unless we flee . . . But where? O grief! . . . I dare not stay!"

News of my plan to flee spread far and wide:
Around the gate my wife and children cried
"Come back! Come back!" Their sorry shrieks brought out
A crowd of anxious friends who milled about
The village square. While one – sincere and sad –
Counselled my wife, another called me mad:
Some cursed, some laughed, some held me up to coarse
Abuse, or planned to hold me down by force.
A few pursued – prepared to seize and bind me . . .
But soon I left our village fields behind me,
Eager to find the path to sure salvation,
And pass the narrow gate, beyond all condemnation.

Pushkin the Narrative Poet

FROM 'POLTAVA'

*The narrative poem 'Poltava', written in praise of
Peter the Great, commemorates the defeat of Sweden
in the battle of that name (1721)*

Dedication

This is for you – but will you hear
My faint and melancholy Muse?
Should distant longing cause you fear?
And will your gentle soul refuse
To read a poet's dedication?
Could it confront a bolted door;
As once a lover's declaration
Remained unanswered, long before?
Listen awhile: the chords I played
Were dear to you, in days gone by:
And now, by cunning fate betrayed,
On one dear joy I still rely:
Your latest words are always mine –
Though dreary parting came at last:
Treasured within a sacred shrine,
They hold my soul forever fast.

Who Rides so Swiftly . . . ?

A loyalist risks his life to reveal the treacherous plans of Mazepa,
Hetman of the Ukrainian Cossacks. He will reach the Russian camp,
but his news will be rejected as 'disinformation' . . .

Who rides so swiftly through the night
When only moon and stars give light?
The steppe is wide, the journey long,
The Cossack bold, the courser strong;

The rider neither stays nor stops
In open field or shady copse;
Northward he goes – with no delay,
Though swirling rivers bar the way.

His damask blade is sharp and bright
As glass; his purse is out of sight.
His charger never seems to tire –
With flowing mane and heart of fire.

An envoy needs a purse of gold:
A cutting blade protects the bold;
The horseman loves his fiery steed –
His Cossack cap is dear indeed.

To save the cap he'll gladly trade
His horse, his purse and cutting blade.
To keep his cap he'll spend his breath
And only loose his grip in death.

That cap of fur! What can it hide?
A deadly letter sewn inside;
And soon the Tsar will have good reason
To strike Mazepa down for treason.

Execution!

Kochubey and Iskra are two loyalists, put to death for opposing
Mazepa's plan to ally the Ukraine with Sweden.

Soldiers stand on stiff parade.
Gleaming lancers canter past.
Hearts and drums are thumping fast.
Hats are motley. Crowds invade
The twisting road and make it writhe
Like a coiling serpent's tail.
See the scaffold – where the blithe
And ever-eager headsman paces . . .
Longing to see his victims' faces.
Playing the tricks that never fail,
He strokes the axe, with pale fastidious
Fingers, banters with the mob in hideous
Humour. Curses, laughter, yelling,
Blend into a ghastly swelling
Sound: but then a sudden shout
Stops the clamour. All is still.
Solemn silence reigns – until
Horses' hooves are heard. Look out!
See the haughty Hetman ride
Flanked by guards in Cossack pride!
Brother, look the other way:
Down the road from Kiev – a cart
Trundles . . . Watch, my friend, and pray!
There he sits, with humble heart,
Reconciled, at rest, believing:
Pious, guiltless Kochubey!
Iskra too, resolved, ungrieving,
Like a lamb for sacrifice.
Now the wagon stops: they hear
Solemn chanting, deep and loud.

Incense rises. All the crowd
Prays in silence – may their dear
Souls repose in paradise!
They in turn forgive their foes.
The silent victims take their places.
First Kochubey – the sacred sign
Is made – he lies upon the block
Before a sea of silent faces ...
They glimpse the axe . . . it gleams . . . it falls.
The head flies off. They groan in shock.
The grass is tainted, bloody red . . .
It seemed to wink, that second head . . .
The happy butcher, nothing loth,
With glee that thrills and yet appals,
Picks up the heads: he grips the hair
Tight in his hand, and shakes them both
Above the crowd who stand and stare . . .

The deed is done. The people scatter.
Straggling home – forgetful folk –
They pass the time in heedless chatter,
Grumbling about the peasant's yoke.
But now, against the motley flow,
Towards the thinning field of death,
A pair of struggling women go;
Dusty, gasping, out of breath:
A fearful mother, anguished daughter
Hurrying to seek the place of slaughter.
"Too late" – they hear a stranger say.
"All over!" Who would wish to stay?
 The fatal stage is torn apart:
A black-robed priest is praying still,
And Cossacks – working with a will –
Are loading coffins on a cart.

Pushkin the Dramatic Poet

FROM 'RUSALKA' – A PLAY

Tsar Nicholas I appointed himself as the poet's personal censor and suggested that he should re-write the tragedy 'Boris Godunov' as a novel in the style of Sir Walter Scott. The poet thought otherwise.

Pushkin's power as a dramatic poet is made plain in his use of blank verse. 'Rusalka' begins with a speech by the Miller, who has used his daughter as a bait to attract the interest of the Prince.

On the bank of the Dnieper: a mill

The Miller
God bless my soul! You girls are all the same.
Plain stupid: just suppose a decent fellow
Comes along – no fool, a man worth having:
At least you ought to know the right approach –
Namely: modest, sensible behaviour!
You lead him on and put him off again:
With 'love-me-do' and 'touch-me-not': and sometimes,
Now and then – just by the way of course –
You drop a hint of marriage . . . taking care
To keep your maiden modesty intact
That's your priceless treasure, so to speak.
Remember, once it's lost it's gone for ever.
And even if there's not a chance of marriage . . .
Never mind, there's profit to be made
For you – and family too. You've got to think . . .
"But will he go on loving me for ever,

Am I his little dove for keeps?" some day-dream
Makes you lose your heads – and reputations . . .
Turns you into sentimental fools – quite ready
To give the fellow what he wants for nothing;
Hang round his neck all day – "your dearest darling . . ."
But as for dearest darling – where's he gone?
He's left you in the lurch – he's upped and vanished . . .
And what's to show for it? You're all so stupid!
I must have made it plain a hundred times . . .
O daughter, do take care. Don't be so dense!
Don't throw away your chance of happiness.
I know you want to keep the prince, but still
You mustn't let him wreck your life . . . What's happening?
You sit and sit and cry and cry for something
That won't come back.

Daughter
But why?
What makes you think
The prince has left me?

The Miller
Why? You ask me why?
How often did he come? Just once a week?
Every day the good Lord sends we'd see him
Here at the mill, and sometimes twice a day.
But now it's less and less – I reckon nine full days
Have come and gone without him. Think of that . . .

Daughter
He's busy. Don't you understand? He's busy . . .
He doesn't have a mill – he can't make water
Help him out. I've often heard him say
That no one works as hard as princes do . . .

The Miller

That's rich. A prince's work? What sort of work?
Chasing hares and foxes – that's their job.
Plus feasting, sending insults to their neighbours,
And whispering fibs to silly girls like you . . .
Him? Hard at work! It breaks my heart to hear it . . .
And as for water helping me . . . Good grief . . .
I get no leisure, day or night: just look!
I've mending jobs to do all round the place . . .
What with rot, and leaking roofs . . . I wish
This prince of yours could fix a few days leave,
Come over here and help us with repairs . . .

Pushkin the Visionary

THE PROPHET

*Here the poet, often described as 'the Russian Byron', puts on the
prophetic mantle and compares his calling to that of the prophet
Isaiah, whose lips were touched with a flaming coal by a seraph in
the Temple in Jerusalem*

I wandered, parched in mind and heart,
Across the desert, gloomy, grim . . .
And where the roadways meet and part
I faced the six-winged seraphim.

With gentle pinions, soft as sleep,
He brushed my eyelids. Wide and deep
My vision grew, prophetic-sighted,
Keen as an eagle, fierce, affrighted!
And then he touched my trembling ear:
What din, what clanging did I hear . . .
Sensing the shuddering of the sky,
Dim shapes that glide beneath the deeps,
The flight of angels, heaven-high,
The growing vine that buds and creeps.
Close to my mouth his fingers lay –
The cunning tongue he tore away
(So foolish, idle, full of lies)
Then his right hand, all bloody-red,
Implanted in my speechless head
The sting that arms the serpent wise!
Last, with a sword he sliced apart
My breast, drew out the flaming heart,
And in the space where once it beat
He thrust a coal – O flaming heat!
I lay exhausted – like the slain –
Till God commanded: "Rise again!
See, Prophet! Hear, and understand!
Obey! The word, which you proclaim,
In wanderings far, by sea and land
Shall set the human heart aflame!"

Pushkin the Friend

TO YAZYKOV

(from Mikhailovskoye, 1824)

The poet-in-exile recalls happier days, goes as far as he dare in criticising the Tsarist autocracy, and looks back with pride to the achievements of his African ancestor, Abram Petrovich Gannibal, a favourite of Peter the Great.

We happy poets always choose
To form a league of joy – united
Offspring of the sacred Muse,
By common themes and flames excited.
Kinship and loyal love we share
Though fate may keep us far apart:
By Ovid's ghost I now declare
That you and I are one in heart!
Yazykov, friend, I'd love to take
The Dorpat road at break of day;
With heavy staff in hand, I'd make
My way towards your friendly dwelling:
There, revived, refreshed, I'd stay
(What carefree stories we'd be telling!)
With talk to set my soul on fire,
And chords from your harmonious lyre!
But Wilful Power has shown its hand,
And fate has blown a blast of sorrow,

Making me wander through the land;
Who knows where I shall sleep tomorrow?
Pursued – in lonely sequestration,
Dragging my fettered days along:
I send this heartfelt invitation.
Dear poet, do not do me wrong.
I long to see you: even here,
Where Peter's former nurseling pined
I mean my Arab forbear – dear
To Tsars – yet quickly out of mind.
He soon forgot the white-and-gold,
Elizabeth's deceitful splendour,
Through lonely summers, damp and cold,
Beneath the shady lime trees, tender
Thoughts of his home would cast a spell . . .
O Africa . . . my hut is ready:
There my brother, sure and steady,
(Yes, you know the rascal well)
Will surely hug you long and hard.
Our wise, inspired, prophetic bard –
Delvig, of course – will play his part.
And thus our trinity will bless
The distant exile's dark distress.
We'll fool the prying state patrol,
And shout for freedom, love and truth.
In noisy banquets we'll extol
The glories of our wayward youth.
With clinking glass and measured verse
We'll cheer each other loud and long,
And hold at bay the winter's curse
With warming wine and rousing song.

Pushkin the Enemy

INSECTS ON DISPLAY

*Pushkin engaged in furious paper warfare with hostile writers.
Here he pins down his critics.*

*"What tiny cattle greet our eyes!
Some are scarcely pinhead-size" – Krylov*

This insect box – a fine collection –
Merits my colleagues' close inspection.
It's colourful – without a doubt.
Where did I dig the rascals out?
And which is which – now, can you guess?
The ladybird? Try Glinka? Yes!
The spider – Kachenovsky – plainly:
Svinin's the beetle, black, ungainly.
Olin? A creeping ant? – the same!
Rayitch – some bug without a name . . .
So many! Lucky lad I am!
Under clear glass I stuck them in,
Pierced with a neat and personal pin –
Just to inspire an epigram.

*Krylov (1769 – 1844), a contemporary of Pushkin,
was a writer of fables*

POEMS IN SCOTS

THE PETITION OF THE GREY HORSE, AULD DUNBAR

by William Dunbar

presented and perhaps performed before King James IV at Stirling (1509?)

adapted and partly translated

"Largesse at Yule!" The cry is loud.
Should a puir palfrey not be proud?
Fillies that carry laird and loon
Expect tae get their hansel soon.
Sir, never let it in toon be tauld
That Yuletide left me in the cauld.

When I was young and strang and spry
I cast up capers tae the sky:
I had been bocht in realmis by
Had I consentit tae be sauld:
Sir, never let it in toon be tauld
That Yuletide left me in the cauld.

With royal steeds I'm feart tae sip,
For if I dae, I feel the whip:
Tae coalheavers then I maun skip,
That crabbit are – and bent – and auld . . .
Sir, never let it in toon be tauld
That Yuletide left me in the cauld.

Tho' I may not be stabled near
Coursers new dressed in silken gear,
My plea is humble and sincere:
In some wee hoose tae be installed.
Sir, never let it in toon be tauld
That Yuletide left me in the cauld.

Suppose I fell frae kingly favour,
Shot forth through field tae pull the claver;
Had I the strength of all Strathnaver,
At Yule I wad be fed and stalled.
Sir, never let it in toon be tauld
That Yuletide left me in the cauld.

I am an auld horse, as ye knaw,
That ever in dule does drag and draw.
Yon court horse drives me frae the straw
Tae thole the fog by firth and and fauld.
Sir, never let it in toon be tauld
That Yuletide left me in the cauld.

I hae run lang on mony a field
Owre pastures that are plain and peeled,
Ye see my scars are scarcely healed:
My puir auld back is bare and bald.
Sir, never let it in toon be tauld
That Yuletide left me in the cauld.

My mane – alas – is turned tae white.
When ither beasts had bran tae bite
I got dry grass. And whae's tae blame?
Whaur can I gae tae hide my shame?
Sir, never let it in toon be tauld
That Yuletide left me in the cauld.

I never yet was gi'en a stable:
My life has been sae miser - able!
My hide tae sell is all I'm able.
Guid maisters, are ye no' appalled?
Sir, never let it in toon be tauld
That Yuletide left me in the cauld.

But should I die your court within
(And surely that would be a sin!)
Let nae the souters get my skin
And cast my innards in the bin . . .
Sir, never let it in toon be tauld
That Yuletide left me in the cauld.

This court has made my poor hert cool.
I'm naething but a broken mule;
And yet . . . new trappings at this Yule
Would make me glad and brave and bauld.
Sir, never let it in toon be tauld
That Yuletide left me in the cauld.

The King's Reply

After our writing, Tresaurer,
Tak in this grey horse, auld Dunbar,
Whilk, as I ken, with service true,
In lyart changed is of hue.
Gar house him noo against this Yuill,
And busk him like a Bishop's mule.
For with my haund I hae endost
Tae pay whitever his trappings cost.

(the original is in **Scottish Poetry from Barbour to James VI** ed.
M.M. Gray, London, J.M. Dent and Sons)

THE LAIRD'S HOMECOMING

Adapted from Pushkin's poem 'Voevoda' – 'The Baron's Return' – see page 245.

"Brither be quick. The maister's hame.
It's him! I see the Laird . . .
He left his horse beside the gate.
He hurryin' through the yaird."

The laird ran up the crooked stair –
His fowk were filled wi' dread.
He pu'd the velvet curtain doon
Tae find . . . an empty bed.

"I've ridden far tae guard the land
Ye were tae guard the hoose.
Noo I come back tae find baith wife
And watchdog on the loose.

Why div ee stand and gape, my man?
Whae daurs disgrace my name?
Gae bring your gun and follow me
Tae hunt for evil game."

Then man and maister made their way
Beneath the glimmering moon;
The pair o' hunters crouched and crept
And found the quarry soon,

Beyond the brae beside the dyke.
A woman wi' a man
Stood sadly face tae face – and then
The bitter words began:

"I loved ye weel. I loved ye lang . . .
Ye tuik the baron's gold.
I cam wi' honour faith and hope
Tae find ye bought and sold."

"The grim auld Laird cam riding by
We had the rent tae pay
My feither frowned, my mither wept:
I couldnae say them nay."

"The Laird has caught ye, flesh and bluid.
Ye'll never see me mair.
I'll seek the wars in Germany
My hert will aye be sair."

Behind the dyke the angry laird
Spake tae the trembling loon:
"Listen. Ye leave the man tae me,
But shoot the woman doon."

"Maister, I'll ride through Liddlesdale,
Follow the English frae,
Or stand alane tae guard your back,
But this I cannae dae.

Ye ken I'm no a skilfu' shot.
My airm – I feel a cramp . . .
The biting breeze has made me weep
I fear the powder's damp."

"I ken your mither cannae pay
For hoose or byre or land.
How daur a snivelling fuil defy
His maister's plain command?

I tell ye: shoot. Ye hear me, shoot."
At last the lad obeyed.
The lovers, in each ithers airms,
Stood still, aghast, afraid.

The cruel musket shook and smoked.
The aim was guid indeed:
The Laird lay low. The lad had shot
His maister through the heid.

A VOTE OF THANKS TO THE STAFF OF TREATMENT ROOM B AT THE BEATSON ONCOLOGY CENTRE, GLASGOW

Ladies,
Ye proved an inspiration
Tae me, whae lairned – wi' consternation
O' prostate cancer's infiltration –
A prospect drearie!
Thanks tae your happy dedication
I'm feelin' cheerie.

First at the desk, wi' smiling face,
Ye welcome every anxious case
And introduce us tae the place
Where Science reigns,
Wi' pooer – we hope – tae track and chase
Oor fears and pains.

Then, in your den, yon big machine
(The like o' which was never seen
In Sauchiehall Street or Glesga Green)
Flashin' and winkin',
Pits me in mind of Hallowe'en.
I've finished drinkin'

Twae cups o' watter – by request.
Let radiation dae the rest.
I ken ye try yer skillfu' best,
And fear nae ill . . .
Buzz . . . hum . . . and buzz . . . I've passed the test
O' lyin' still!

We stayed the course for eight lang weeks
And noo my humble poem speaks
(Jist gie me time tae fix ma breeks
And finish dressing)
A million thanks – wi' nae critiques –
God gie ye's blessing.

THE TOAST TO THE LASSIES

At the Scots Night, Riverside Drama Club, Stirling,
February 20th 2009

Guid friends! Ye ken I'm no' a moaner;
But my puir heart was turned tae stone
A ton in weight: she made me groan
A hauf hour lang.
"Ye'll toast the lassies" said Fiona,
"In word or sang."

Fiona, dear, I'll dae my best
Tae pass your 'Toast the lassies!' test.
My lines, (tho' weel enough expressed
Tae raise a smile)
Can nivver match – in skill or zest –
Yon Lad frae Kyle.

But still this truth I cannae hide:
My lovely wife is aye my guide.
We face the telly, side by side,
Then aff we toddle
Tae comfy bed – and thus provide
A guid role model.

In younger days I felt sae happy
Tae change the bonnie bairn's wet nappy . . .
I'll sae nae mair . . . let's make it snappy:
Fast forward years
O' school, with chalk and talk and strap (ye
Mind thae fears

And joys?) It's time tae think o' 'queans
A' plump and straping in their teens' . . .
But noo cauld conscience intervenes.
And says "Bad lad!
"Ye'd luik a fuil in skin tight jeans:
Ye daft auld dad!

Whit's mair, ye're noo a granddad tae!
I tell ye whit ye've got tae dae:
Compose that poem, song or lay
Tae blow the mind;
And sing the best that man can say
O' womankind."

Sae here we go: "Braw Lads, arise!
Ye Balding Heids, lift up your eyes!
Declare the truth that nane denies,
Sober or drunk:
Withoot the women's enterprise
We males are sunk.

Likewise, each Senior Cit - i - zen:
Jist whit tae dae fu' weel ye ken,
When Scots Night rumbles roond again.
Let's raise oor glasses
(We modest, wise, well-meaning men)
And toast the lassies."

THE LASSIES' REPLY

For much of the time in the tale of MANkind
The roles of the sexes were plainly defined:
The male was the master – his powers were unflagging,
While females made headway by charming – or nagging.

Small boys were created from snails or from frogs
(For so says the rhyme), or the tails of young dogs;
While maidens consisted of sugar and spice
And grew up to be Nice – or Devoted to Vice.

SHE toiled a warm bedroom and kitchen to keep
As a place for her man to relax or to weep.
HE laboured the bread and the bawbees to win –
And was sooner excused if suspected of sin.

On the head of our Bard – we must sadly admit –
The cap of these facts is discovered to fit:
Though his skill as a poet our wonder arouses,
Jean Armour declared that he needed two spouses.

But now things have changed, and we women have come
To preach in the pulpit – and shove in the scrum.
We are learning to give just as good as we get,
And some of the fellas may feel under threat.

Don't worry, dear menfolk: there's no need to fear
The satires of Sonntag, the strictures of Greer,
In Riverside Drama the thing is the play –
And wonderful women hold merciful sway.

No names need be mentioned – you see them around:
Without them what panto could get off the ground?
So please be upstanding and drink to the dream:
Our lads and our lasses . . .
     . . . will work as a team.

IN MEMORY OF ELLIOT RENWICK, BANDMASTER, THE SALVATION ARMY, HAWICK (MAY 12, 2006)

Farweel guid freend – and loyal Teri.*
The final lap was hard and weary.
But this ah dinnae need tae query:
Tae age frae youth
Ee served the Maister, no' in theory,
But simple truth.

His words and deeds were aye befor ee.
Nae doot the gracious King o' Glory
Is weel acquaintit wi' the story:
Wi' stick in hand,
*Molto con brio, con amore*** –
Ee led the band.

Dear Prince of Peace, accept oor prayer.
Hae Margaret's Elliot in eer care:
Hei wiz an active lad – aware –
At hand when needed.
Sae help iz promise . . . and prepare
Tae serve . . . as hei did.

> ** a 'Teri' is a native of Hawick*
> *** 'in great style, with much love*

AND FINALLY . . .

HELPFUL SUGGESTIONS!

I need breakfast – I need bed –
I need a kiss for a bump on my head –

I need Krinkly Krunkly chips –
I need a space ship for afternoon trips –

I don't need your old cassettes –
I do need dad – to mind my pets.

I need a rubber – I need mum –
I need the answer to a horrible sum –

I need a jumbo ice-cream cone –
I need a private bully-free zone –

I need a dream that's gotta come true –
I need the Universe – I need YOU.

IN PRAISE OF STICKY TAPE

This present comes from me to you
To tell you that my heart is true.
Observe the clear adhesive tape –
Its colour, sticking power and shape!
It's shape is round: it knows no end –
Just like our perfect love, dear friend!
Its STICKING POWER will rarely fail:
Let STICKABILITY prevail
Between us still! Its colour – clear –
Implies true love need never fear:
TRANSPARENT TRUTH beyond all price
Is ours – and this is extra nice:
What tender care you get from me!
I paid for two – and got one free.

271